NOT MY FATE

Caitlin Press Inc.

8100 Alderwood Road, Halfmoon Bay, BC V0N 1Y1
www.caitlin-press.com

Text design and cover design by Vici Johnstone
Printed in Canada

Caitlin Press Inc. acknowledges financial support from the Government of Canada and the Canada Council for the Arts, and the Province of British Columbia through the British Columbia Arts Council and the Book Publisher's Tax Credit.

Canada Council   Conseil des Arts   BRITISH COLUMBIA   Funded by the   Canada
for the Arts   du Canada   ARTS COUNCIL   Government
                                                              of Canada

Library and Archives Canada Cataloguing in Publication

Romain, Janet, author

     Not my fate : the story of a Nisga'a survivor / Janet Romain.

Issued in print and electronic formats.

ISBN 978-1-927575-54-3 (paperback).—ISBN 978-1-927575-61-1 (epub)

     1. Caplin, Josephine. 2. Niska Indians—Canada--Biography.
3. Abused women—Canada—Biography. 4. Native peoples—Canada—Residential schools. I. Title.

E99.N734R64 2016   305.4092   C2016-903634-0
                                          C2016-903635-9

JANET ROMAIN

Not My Fate

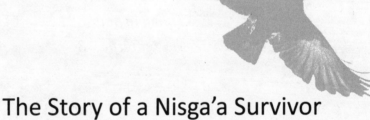

The Story of a Nisga'a Survivor

CAITLIN PRESS

Contents

*This book is dedicated to to all those who refuse
to be defined by the hardships of life.*

Preface

Everyone lives a story. Sometimes challenges are set when we are very young and if our lives are about rising to our challenges and overcoming them, then some stories are more compelling than others.

That is how I feel about the story in this book. The woman I call Jo was born into a tough situation with serious problems and how she deals with them and with her life has inspired me to record the pertinent facts. I hope I have taken good care of her story.

I am a Métis Canadian and proud of it. I learned a lot writing this book and I think there is still a lot Canadians need to know in order to reconcile history with our lives today.

NOTE: The events in this book are true, except where I have fictional-ized Martha's and Sarah's stories in an attempt to fill in the gaps created by the lack of historical records. The fiction stories are indicated by a * character. The names in this book have been changed to protect the privacy of the people involved.

Jo

The frantic barking of the dogs alerts me and I go to the window to watch as a small green car drives up the road to our house. I've been expecting them for some time: supper is ready and keeping warm in the oven. When Jo phoned me this morning she didn't know how long it would take to drive here, so I made lasagna—it loses nothing by sitting in the oven. The two women get out of the car and Jo comes to meet us, big smile and ready hugs.

She's got on a straw garden hat, the brim remodelled with black lace trim. Her two long, salt and pepper braids are hanging over the shoulder of her short denim jacket, and her long print skirt has work-boots peeking out at the bottom. She's wearing her carved eagle neck-lace that I keep remaking for her: she always wears it. The eagle was carved out of a bone by another friend—Eagle is her clan. Her face is round with heavy, dark eyebrows arching above dark brown sparkly eyes, and she has a huge wide smile.

She introduces us to her friend whose car they came in. "This is my friend, Maria." Maria smiles and holds out her hand. "So nice to meet you, I've heard so much about you both," she says.

"Oh God, what has she told you? It might be all lies!" I grin at Maria.

She protests "Just good stuff. Don't worry." We all laugh and make our way in.

My husband, Rick, and I have been waiting for them to get here so we can eat with them. I serve supper right away; the table has been set for an hour. The wait has made the lasagna hold together nicely.

I serve it with a salad, all the ingredients picked fresh today. We eat in relative silence till we're full. Maria sighs. "That was so good! Thanks so much."

"There's dessert," I say and Jo groans. "Why didn't you tell me before I ate so much? Oh well, I'll find another corner to tuck it into. Bring it on! I never turn down dessert." She rubs her stomach and giggles.

After supper, Jo and I clean up while Rick and Maria go outside to have a smoke. Jo explains why she quit her job.

"I simply couldn't do it anymore, Janet. My friggin' hands, they're seizing up. They get cramps in them so bad, I can't do anything. Sometimes they hurt so much by night, I go to sleep whimpering. I don't know what's wrong with them. I can't work. I could hardly make the beds anymore, I couldn't pack dishes, I feel so useless. Look at them—look how they only bend."

She's right, they sure don't bend much. On the right hand, the middle finger and the baby finger hardly bend at all. The fact that she's complaining about them is unusual: it's more like her to pretend everything's fine, even if it's not. I know better than to suggest she take some medication for the pain. She doesn't do medication except in extreme circumstances, although this hand thing does seem to fit the bill. "What's wrong with them? Why are they like that?" I ask.

"I don't know. Sometimes when they cramp up it's so painful it brings tears to my eyes." Jo's round brown face crumples, and it looks like she's going to break into the promised tears right now. I know it's more than the pain of her hands; she's got more worries than that. I don't like pity parties, not my own, not anybody's. I try to lighten things up, to reassure her. "Day by day. Just wait a bit. They'll most likely get better when you've had a chance to rest them. It was probably working too hard; you maybe need to find a job that's easier to do."

She shakes her head. "That wasn't exactly a hard job. I've done a lot harder things than that before. It was nothing like running a chainsaw, and I did that plenty. No, something's for sure wrong. I'm gonna go see a doctor when I get home; find out what it is."

"That's good, at least you'll find out how to fix them." I feel phony, talking false optimism. I have no more faith than Jo in the medical system, and she's had trouble with her hands and wrists for years now. Her first operations for carpal tunnel on her wrists happened when she was still in her twenties, and I know she only goes to the doctor if she's in dire pain. She's more likely to research herbal cures and go that route.

Maria plays guitar. She brings it in, and Jo requests a song that she explains is a Maria original, written to her children. It's very good, I think; I look at Rick to see what he thinks. He is so much more aware of musical composition than I am. He nods approval, and goes to get his own guitar. He starts playing; Maria stops him, shakes her head and asks, "What is that chord? Right there—what is that?" Soon they've launched into technical stuff that Jo and I zone out on. We sit close together and chat while they play and sing. They sound good together. Maria has a good voice with carrying power, a little raspy on the low end, and she harmonizes well with Rick. Jo and I clap after every song.

Rick and Maria move to the music room around the corner from the kitchen table so Rick can plug in. Jo says, "Show me the garden, Janet! We'll have a quick tour before it gets dark, okay? Quick now!!" I'm fast to agree. We are kindred spirits when it comes to gardens, and we can go on for hours.

Jo, Maria, and I are all mixed blood. The Native blood is thin in me, but it's there nonetheless. One of my grandmothers was Métis: her family chose to hide their identity among the immigrant population, on purpose. "I am French; came over on the boat when I was a young girl," was what my grandma said to me. "Un, deux, trois...." She would count to ten in French. I don't know if she ever believed otherwise. I don't understand how she could overlook her birth certificate from North Dakota, but maybe she knew and simply wasn't telling. There were better historians in the family who remembered, who whispered to all the children that we were Métis, and that Grandma Pépin was full-blood Cree. Another whispered that she was Anishinabe, but all agreed that she was Native. What pride that gave me as a child, to know I was part Indian too, and told the truth of it by no less of an authority than my own father.

Jo is half-Native, half-German. She's very good looking, short and curvy, and she wears her hair long, usually braided. She used to have a pretty healthy dark moustache as well, one that stayed on long after removal became stylish. My sister and I used to bug her, and call her a wussie when she refused to have it ripped off her lip like we were doing. I remember the first time she had it waxed; she was at my sister's house, and she thought Rene was sad. Jo always wants to make everyone feel good: she wants to fix things, to make everyone laugh. That day Rene's daughter, Bev, who had just completed a beautician's course, was visiting as well, and when my sister went out to do chores, Jo asked Bev to wax her moustache. "For Rene," she said. She's waxed it ever since. Jo has a knock-out figure: she wears tight jeans and short tops—no muffin top hanging over there!

Maria is a big girl: she drinks big, eats big, lives her life big. She is also half-Native, with dark skin and hair and eyes. Her hair is curly, and there's lots of it. She is the kind of person people instinctively like, and she takes on life with a hearty laugh.

Both Jo and Maria have Native mothers and white fathers. Both their families could at best be called dysfunctional; Jo's parents both alcoholics, with one of them missing her whole life, and Maria's father was a convicted pedophile, her mother somehow unable to protect herself or the children. That doesn't mean that they were dysfunctional in every way. Jo loves her dad: he was an adequate father in many ways, and in her memory he is good. She told me, "Janet, I was raised with love. We were happy once. Our family was happy—me and Sam and Dad and Uncle. There was love in our house: they *loved* us. It was enough to go around."

I don't know how Maria feels about her father. She helped take him to court and get him convicted, so I don't imagine she has too much respect for him. They are two different things, love and respect. If they go hand in hand it's a wonderful thing, but most the time the two aren't quite touching.

Jo says it's inside you, and it's partly what you remember—what you believe—that makes you Native or not. She says some people are only red on the outside, calls them apples. She thinks there is a genetic memory built into the very cells that compose our bodies as well as a spirit that can't be defined by colour or race; both giving us our attitudes. She believes we are born again and again, and right now we are being the bridges, neither white nor Native, the left side of us not biting the right.

My ancestors hid our heritage, thanks to their colouring, which was light enough to be dark-skinned French. It was hidden well enough that the edict from the Canadian government putting every Native, Métis, and Inuit child in residential schools far from their homes and the love and protection of their families, bypassed us completely. Thank you, Ancestors.

For Jo's and Maria's families, that law was devastating. Jo's mother is from Kincolith, now called Gingolx. It was originally the Place of Skulls, the name commemorating a pre-Contact skirmish. Kincolith is on the north shore of the Nass estuary, close to the southern tip of Alaska where it drapes down the BC coastline. It was settled in 1867 by an Anglican church mission, meant to be a fully Christian society with twenty-five or thirty founding members. In the next thirteen years, the town population grew to 200. The smallpox that spread itself around that same period never visited Kincolith, likely because of its isolation, yet its absence was easily attributed to the Lord God Almighty by the religious. The Anglicans opened a school in town as soon as possible and provided education, mostly religious study— religion being one of the cornerstones of the Native world. The Europeans called the local religion "superstition," "pagan ritual," and "nonsense," deemed it "savage" and were determined to stamp it out and replace it with Jesus.

Maria's family is from the Hazeltons which are called that because there are three distinct towns. They are differentiated by calling one South Town, which is across the river from Old Town and used to be connected by a foot bridge, and then there is the one on the highway called New Town. I don't know much about Maria's mother, but I know her generation was the culmination of the effects of residential schools and that they saw the end of them. I know a bit more about Maria's father: he hurt a lot of people, and his family was no exception to the rule. He was a predator, always looking for his next victim.

One day Jo was listening to the radio and someone was saying they would like a list of convicted pedophiles posted in their town for the safety of their children. Jo got all worked up, with tears in her eyes. She heartily agreed with the speaker. "Cuz, they don't stop just because they've been convicted and spent a few months in jail. They don't stop. Nobody comes out of jail fixed: they go on to hurt people again and again. They never stop! In fact, it almost seems to give them a licence to do it again, like they say to themselves and to society, 'It's a sickness. I can't help it.' To give themselves permission. I tell you, Janet, they should lock those people up, castrate them, brand their foreheads, so everyone can see what they are and steer clear of them." Strong, bitter words from my peace-loving friend. At the time I thought it so out of character, so much hatred reserved for those who would molest children, but feeling a bit that way myself, at the time I didn't think any more of it.

Jo's earliest memories are from the bush. Her dad and uncle were horse loggers, and they lived in a line camp. Everything was on skids: the little line-shack where they bunked, the cookhouse, and the horses' barns with mangers. The men got up before it was light, lit the coal oil lamp, and added wood to the tin heater in the centre of the cabin. Jo remembers the security she felt, curled up with her brother, Sam, watching while the men layered wool pants with suspenders over wool long johns, topped off with heavy coats and black toques. She remembers the smile at the door before they went off to the cookhouse to eat their breakfast. She remembers the warmth of the wood fire and the glow of the kerosene lamp. The men fed the horses before they went for breakfast, and daybreak would find the horses already harnessed and dancing with impatience. Jo liked the way the horses' breath looked in the morning, big clouds of steam coming from each nostril as they pranced, seemingly anxious to get to work. She liked seeing them come plodding home at dark, steam rolling off them in a cloud. She used to perch on the manger while her dad took off the harness and rubbed them down with a rag, then brushed them fluffy and covered them with a blanket.

Jo and Sam usually got up in time to see them leave in the morning; after the men left was the time the children could go for breakfast because they weren't supposed to be in the way of the men. There were lots of men in the camp and only one woman, the cook. Jo and Sam were only supposed to bother her if there was an emergency. The men logged during the daylight hours, and they played cards and drank whiskey at night. Jo remembers going to sleep while the men played, the air a blue haze from all the cigarette smoke. She doesn't have any memory of her mother. Sometimes she thinks about a round brown face surrounded by long hair and smiling at her, but she thinks it's more imagination than memory.

Jo says, "I used to wonder sometimes, how a mother could just get up and walk away from her kids? It wasn't just us—she had three kids already who she left before us. I have a half-sister named Trina, and a half-brother named James, and they have a brother named Don."

"What do you mean, 'they have a brother'? Isn't he your brother too?"

"I guess so. When I was younger I always wondered, how could she do it? Leave us behind? My father tried to get her back; he went to Rupert and I know he saw her. I used to be so mad at her, thinking she must have not liked us."

"Have you met your sister?"

"Not yet. I talked to Trina on the phone, and she sent me fish. I'm going up there to meet her one of these days."

"Does she remember your mother?"

"Yeah. More than I do. Which doesn't mean much because anything is more than zero! Everybody in Rupert knew my mom. It was like a small town where everyone knows everyone. It's sad when I think about it now; strangers knew my mother better than I did. But what I'm trying to tell you about is that I'm not mad at her anymore. I feel sorry for her, and I wish I knew who she was inside. I know she wasn't very strong, not strong enough."

Jo's voice goes deep, and she goes and stands by the window, leans her forehead on the glass, and speaks very quietly. "I was listening to the radio, and a woman was on there talking about her experiences in residential school. Then I had this awful feeling that there was a connection between what that woman was saying and my mother. I got on the phone right away, called my sister, and asked her if Mom went to residential school, When she said, 'Yes,' I wasn't even surprised. Then I knew she couldn't help it, just like that woman on the radio, she couldn't help it. She didn't know anything about being a mother because she didn't get one herself. Instead of a mother she got a cold old school."

Jo didn't have a mother, but she had her brother, Sam. Sam was the one who always looked out for Jo. When the adults were all on the sauce it was Sam who made sure his little sister got her food, Sam who got her clothes out and helped her get dressed, and Sam who tied her shoes. They were a pair, two small Native children weaving their way through childhood hand in hand. They shared everything, even slept together. He is there in all her strong childhood memories.

Jo says, "It makes a person wonder, how the things that happen to you as a kid set the stage for the other things that happen. There's this guy on *Oprah*, and he says it's cycles, that everything happens in cycles, and if you want things to go differently you have to break the cycle. Me and Sam, we broke some of the cycles. That's partly what made us strong. You know what my brother did when his kids were young and his old lady was drinking? He used to take his two kids with him when he worked night shift at the sawmill; he made them beds in the car, and they had food if they woke up and were hungry. He'd go out at coffee breaks and lunch hours and check on them. He wasn't letting anyone get to his kids while he wasn't there to protect them. He made sure they were safe. He broke that cycle."

Breaking those cycles is one of the reasons I admire Jo so much. She has an inner strength that makes the best of any situation; she's learned to laugh at a challenge. If she's able to help with anything, she does. She's the person who smiles at strangers and holds the door for them. Her brother breaking the cycle of child abuse could be looked at in an entirely different fashion. If anyone had noticed that a sawmill employee had two kids sleeping in the car in the parking lot it would have seemed mighty strange. Someone would likely have called social services, thinking it was not so much protective as weird, and therein lies a big lesson in judgement.

The bloody research

I research our local history to find out about residential schools. There was a residential school near us on the shore of Fraser Lake. The Lejac Residential School was a huge brick building that opened in 1922 and closed in 1976. It housed Native children from Sai'kuz, Nescoslie, Nad'leh, and Stellat'en, as well as ones from as far away as Lower Post and Atlin. The school was Catholic, and it is a telling point that it was torn down soon after closing. The site commemorates Rose Prince, a Native woman who has posthumously been declared a saint by the Catholic Church.

The research bounces me around, linking into articles and drawing me to previously unknown places. It becomes a nightmare. I read stories from the survivors and I end up in tears in front of the screen. How could any society be so cruel? Not just any society but my own! The Canadian government practised cultural genocide. I can hardly bring myself to believe it, yet it is clearly proven. Not a hidden mandate, but a government proclamation: the church-run Indian Industrial Schools were designed to "kill the Indian in the child" and turn the children into civilized industrial workers who would grow up to spurn their own traditions. The government would accomplish this by taking children as young as four years old from their homes and keeping them in the schools for sometimes as long as a decade. They would not allow the children to see their families, speak their languages, or practise any cultural act. The establishment denigrated everything about their culture. Survivors say they were used as slave labour, abused at the whim of the establishment, and that most teachers were cruel and used physical assault as punishment, something that would never have happened in their homes. I am so ashamed of this part of my country's history; I can hardly believe such a thing could have happened in Canada. We sure didn't learn that in high school history. We learned that our brave European ancestors discovered this land, this empty new world, not that they disrespected the citizens who inhabited the land to the degree that they chose not to see that it was already owned. They didn't discover it, they were shown it by Native guides; Europeans stole the land from people who had lived on it for thousands of years, a society so benign to the earth that after thousands of years their environmental footprint can hardly be found. When this land was "discovered" it had all the resources for life, in spades. "The true north strong and free" indeed!

Some research shows that Canada-wide, half the Native children—conservative estimates say 40 per cent, some say more than 60 per cent—didn't make it through the schools, the most prevalent disease being tuberculosis, TB. According to a 1907 government report by Dr. Peter Bryce, who was the Chief Medical Officer for the Department of Indian Affairs, it was a deliberate, systematic exposure to TB that infected so many children. Biological warfare against children! As if that's not bad enough, it was compounded by a poor diet and prison-like surroundings, completely lacking parental love and affection. Security was more important than the children's well-being, because too many had tried to run. Some died from disease, some were murdered, some died trying to get away, some simply died emotionally in the schools. Survivors say they learned to have no feelings, to be dead inside and not care. They learned to steal, and mostly they'd steal food.

Eventually the web bounces me around to the Port Alberni Residential School. My horror grows: this school had a sexual predator hired as a dorm supervisor, a drunken reverend, a sadistic matron—the school was a frightening nightmare for decades of innocent little children. I get the sick feeling that Jo's mother went to this school, and my nasty suspicion is compounded when I read another man's story. He was only four years old when he was taken from Kincolith to the infamous Alberni Residential School. He lived to testify at the trial of Arthur Henry Plint, the dorm supervisor during his years at school, and then he killed himself.

I try to find the attendance lists for the schools on the web but can't find any trace. The closest I come is a copy of a letter from Access to Information and Privacy: a lady has found her mother's name on the attendance lists of the schools through Section 26 of the *Privacy Act*. Maybe that's the only way to get it. I tell Jo I'm going to make up her mother's story for her. But I have to start with her grandma.

---

* Snatched away

Jo's grandma, Martha, was seven years old in 1923 when they took her from her home to the school. The RCMP snatched her from her mother's arms. Martha held that picture of her mother in her mind for a long time, for the seemingly endless years of residential school—her mother on her knees reaching out to her as the RCMP officer carried her out of sight of her home and all she loved. He put her down so she could walk herself but kept a firm hand on her shoulder all the way down to the harbour, to a big boat where he handed her to another white man who pushed her into the boat's cabin, already filled with small children trying not to cry, and shut the door firmly behind her. Her little cousin was already there, and Martha went over and sat real close. She held her cousin's hand, both giving and taking some small reassurance in the contact. She was so scared herself and her cousin was a lot younger, just a baby really. Martha knew going to school was an awful thing, that something really bad was happening, and there was nothing her mother could do about it. Her *Kookum* said they'd be starved out if she didn't get sent to school this year, that there were more things to think about than one child going to school. "Everybody's children have to go to school. Martha's no different," she'd said. That morning her mother had braided her hair and put in the pretty shells, and Martha was sure she'd seen tears glistening in her mother's eyes. She kept squeezing her too hard, and had kissed her again and again and again.

Eventually the boat pulled away from Kincolith, stopping twice more at other villages to collect yet more silent children. For Martha, it was the longest boat ride she'd ever been on. She didn't get seasick. She'd been out with her mother catching fish lots of times, but some of the other kids weren't so lucky. Everyone tried not to look at the people who were puking. No one came down to clean up the mess. It smelled so bad in the cabin that Martha wanted to go out on deck, but the door was closed and locked. Martha and her cousin huddled together, Martha's robe wrapped around them both, not so much for heat as for security. They'd both cried, silently and unobtrusively, feeling guilty for the tears—only babies cried. They endured the trip in abject misery. When the boat left the channel and faced the full brunt of the Pacific, the misery turned to fear, and all the children cried surreptitious tears of homesickness, fear, and loss.

When the boat eventually docked and the cabin door was opened by a baldheaded clergyman dressed in a black suit, it opened on a pathetic scene of sick and disoriented small children.

"Oh, for the love of the Lord! Smell that stench! For just one time, just once, that's all I ask, Lord, could you let the little savages get here without puking all over the blessed boat?" The black-suited man raised his hands to the air as he delivered his request to his lord, then brought them down and clapped them together loudly; he was rewarded with the full attention of the children.

"Line up," he ordered.

No one moved. "Line up, I say!" he repeated and clapped his hands again. "Boys here. Girls here." He pointed, no one moved. "Blessed little children, you'll be learning to do as you're told soon enough." He roughly grabbed the nearest boy by the shoulder and stood him up by the door, grabbed the next in the same fashion and shoved him behind the first. As he reached for number three child, the move was anticipated. He only had to motion for the next and the lines quickly formed.

I was in my early twenties when I first met Jo. I didn't know it then, but we are almost exactly the same age. At the time I thought she was much younger than me. I was visiting my parents when I met them. She was drop-dead gorgeous and so was her friend. They came with an old friend of my parents, Newt, who'd stopped by for a visit. Both Jo and her friend seemed so young, I thought the two of them must have been getting a ride with him. My mother cast away that assumption the next time I visited.

"But she's so young, and so pretty," I protested.

"And he's so old?" Mom laughed. "He's eight years younger than your father."

"He's still old," I'd replied, from the height of my arrogance. Little did I know back then that age is a matter of perspective, that there are young folks who are already old and old people who will always be young.

The next time I saw Jo was Christmas the following year. She and Newt had spent the summer and fall down at Rock Creek, picking away at a gold claim. Newt wasn't overly ambitious, however he was the holder of grand dreams. The gold mine was one of them.

It sounded like hard work they were doing, but it was more than twenty-five years later that I heard what brutally hard work it really was. It was Newt's kick at the can, but he missed. None of that shows in the photos from that Christmas, though. There are some pictures of me and Jo wrestling in the kitchen, Newt sitting at the big table beside my father, both of them laughing. Neither Jo nor I remember why we were wrestling, but both of us are grinning. I have on a T-shirt dress with a pleated skirt, red inside the pleats and black outside, and she has on denim jeans and a hippy shirt, white cotton with flowers embroidered down the front and two string ties with tiny bells tied in a floppy bow. Her long hair is still black in the photo, and she's so tanned she looks full Native. Newt was a good-looking guy. He didn't have any family up north; they all lived down at the coast. That's how my parents and Newt referred to Ladner, where they all grew up, "The Coast." They said it like it should be capitalized. My parents wouldn't have liked the thought of anyone's spending Christmas alone, so Newt often came to our Christmas festivities.

There are so many things going on inside photos that you have to kind of cast yourself into the picture to get to the sideways part. I remember that Christmas as being extra special for all of us: my older sister and I both returned with our spouses to live in the area after spending a few years in Alberta. There was a feeling in the air of homecoming, and I remember how glad I was to be back.

The picture of Newt shows him smiling into the camera, square faced with blond curly hair—long, according to my dad's standards, whose own hair is properly trimmed above his ears. Newt had his own hippy look happening: hippy chic, not hippy scruffy. He's very buff in the photo, highly defined arm muscles disappearing into a short-sleeved, India import shirt. It's hard to equate the good-looking

Newt in the photo with the Newt of today, mind disappearing into the fog and breath deserting him as he devours an ever-increasing line of cigarettes and beers.

When I showed Jo those two photos—me and her, Newt and Dad, she took off her glasses and held the photo up close to her eyes, reminding me of my friend's mother who has macular degeneration and can only see a photo if she holds it within an inch of one eye. Jo scrunched up her face and stared at the picture for so long I asked, "Do you even remember that?" It took her a while to answer, sometimes she thinks things through a long time. "I was beginning to be strong," she finally said "It was about then that I'd got my epilepsy under control. I was learning who I was."

"Epilepsy? You had epilepsy? Like doing the funky chicken on the floor?"

Jo nodded solemnly.

"Holy crap! Did it go away?"

"Epilepsy isn't something that goes away. It's something you always have; you have to control yourself not to have seizures."

"Control yourself how?"

"Promise not to laugh?"

"I promise."

"It's from smoking pot." Despite the promise I couldn't help it, I laughed. "Really?"

"Really! Since I've started smoking pot I haven't had very many seizures."

"Who told you to do that? Or was it an accidental side effect?" I laughed some more.

"Seriously, way back when, Gramma told me that people used to smoke stuff to stop having seizures. She told me to try smoking pot and I did, and then I didn't have any more seizures. That's when I started smoking. It works; I don't take any other thing for it, and I went from two or three grand mal seizures a week to zero. I had maybe two in the last ten years."

"Whoa! That's impressive. You don't take anything else? What Gramma?"

"Nope. Nothing else. Gramma GreyGrouse. She's my fos-
ter-grandma. Before that, I was on medicine, but it didn't work worth
a damn. It made me stupid and wasn't so good at stopping them. My
brother Sam has epilepsy too, but he won't take medication for it cuz
he remembers how stupid I was when I took the pills."

"I didn't know you had that." I reflected on the one epileptic
seizure I'd witnessed long ago in high school, the frantic effort by the
stricken girl's friend to try and shove the edge of her wallet in between
her teeth (so she wouldn't swallow her tongue? Is that possible?) I
remember the perfect imprints of her teeth on the wallet. Years later,
Rick, whose mother had cared for an impressive forty-six foster children, told me he had a foster sister who was epileptic, and when he
was watching her he always carried a short wooden spoon that he
was to insert between her teeth and tell her to bite at the first sign of
a fit. He thought it was so she wouldn't bite her tongue. That's not
even something that people do now. I ask Jo what it's like to have an
epileptic fit.

"Seizure," she corrects me. "It's called a seizure for a reason, because that's what it does—it seizes you. First it's your eyes: you start
seeing everything strobe, you know, like the light. Bright and dark,
light and dark, holy shit, Janet, don't ask me to imagine how it is, it
makes it too near. I don't want to think about it."

"Sorry."

"It's okay. Sometimes I get that feeling still. I hate that feeling; it
totally controls everything, and it gets me all shaky." Her voice slows
down. "Now when I get this feeling I know to stop what I'm doing
and step back a bit and relax. If I can, I have a smoke right then. As
soon as I can, I do. It works." Jo shrugged, lit up a joint.

Scrubbed and uniformed

You could see the school from the dock. It dominated the landscape,
a four-storey brick building built on the rise of the land. The two-
block walk through town was a welcome relief after the harrowing
trip. Martha held her cousin's hand as they followed the clergyman
through the streets that led to the school. The school was enormous,

the biggest building she'd ever seen. Her wonder grew to match her fear when the clergyman said it was where they were going; all the children walked up the stairs to the entryway wide eyed. They were led into a large room with benches on either side and told to sit down. Martha knew a lot of English because her mother spoke it to some of her friends, and unlike most of the children, Martha had no trouble understanding the commands of the clergy.

The girls were seated on the left of the room and the boys on the right. They were disappearing in groups, four at a time were selected and sent out. When it was Martha and her cousin's turn they rose in unison and went through the door, down a long corridor, and ended up in a bathroom with four galvanized tubs of warm water. There were two women overseeing the bathing. They stripped each of the children at the door and tossed their clothing into a garbage bin. Most of the children were old enough to be embarrassed by public nudity: no one wanted to climb in the tub of water, and certainly no one wanted the oil scrubbed out of their hair. Those who resisted were forced, no match in size for the adults. When the children were sufficiently scrubbed they were lifted out, dried off, and outfitted with school uniforms. They never saw their own clothes again. Then they were lined up at the door of another room where yet another woman set them one by one on a tall stool and cut their hair into a generic cut, just below the ears, straight off, with bangs in front, cut straight off as well. Martha felt like crying but she didn't; she tried to remain stoically impassive when they took the shells from her hair, her beautiful hair that her mother loved braiding, but something inside her crumpled anyway when her hair hit the floor. The school uniform was scratchy, and she kept squirming uncomfortably on the bench where they ended up seated, waiting for the rest of the kids to be processed. When the group was assembled again, minus the boys, they were led down the corridor to the dorm room where two long rows of bunk beds awaited them.

Jo and I talk on the phone one or two times a week. We've been keeping this up for years—she's the earliest riser of all my friends. My friends are mostly really nice people, but if you phone them before a "decent hour," some are not going to act very nice. Jo, on the other hand, is always happy to hear from me even if it's five thirty a.m. and I have woken her up. She can do the same thing to me without my hanging onto offence.

The phone rings once then stops. Sometimes that's her signal to call.

"Oh good. I was hoping you'd figure it out."

"I guessed. What's up?"

"I went to the doctor in Smithers. He referred me to a specialist in Prince George, I have an appointment in January. I've got enough money for the bus ticket to Fort Fraser, but do you think you could drive me into Prince?"

"Yeah," I say. "Can do. Are you going to stay for a while?"

"You want me to?"

"Yep, I want you to. Stay for a couple of weeks." During the winter months Rick spends long hours driving the log truck, and the kids are all busy with their lives, and I'm alone a lot, so I really would appreciate the company.

The Greyhound passenger bus runs twice daily from Rupert, except on Wednesdays, and is sometimes on time, but not this time. It finally pulls in twenty-five minutes late, and Jo is the only passenger whose actual destination is Fort Fraser. Eight other people pile out and light up cigarettes. Jo banters with the driver while he opens the belly of the bus and pulls out her bags. She's loaded to the nines: huge canvas backpack bulging around the laces, duffel bag big enough to pack a hockey player's equipment, and a carry-on almost as heavy as she is. The driver drags out the backpack and comments that it's nearly the weight limit. Jo giggles at him. "Oh, my friend, it's far over the weight limit. We'll have to drag it to the car." The VW Bug with the back hatch open is parked right beside the bus, so he gallantly hauls it over and deposits it in the trunk. I put the duffel bag in on top and Jo tells me to be careful with the carry-on. "It's breakable."

The bus driver calls to her, "See you next time," as we leave.

"It was a harrowing trip," Jo tells me on the ride home. "I sat in the front seat all the way and talked to him. There was a horrible snow storm between Houston and Burns Lake, and we couldn't hardly see the road. We crawled along, but he's a good driver, nice guy too.

Once he came around South Town just so he could drop us off closer to home, and he's not supposed to, you know."

"He was pretty nice about the bags," I say. "What did you pack in there, lead?"

"Wait and see," she says.

At home she greets the dogs by name and pets them, and they respond with wags and licks. She starts unpacking as soon as she gets in the door. The breakable stuff is salmon, canned in pint jars, for her to eat while she's here, she informs us with a grin. There's a government rule: she can't give us fish, but she can bring her own to eat. Wink, wink.

The other heavy stuff is books. Good books, treasures. A Robert Service novel, hard cover. I didn't even know he wrote anything but poetry. I love his poetry; for me the rhythm of his words holds the beat of the north, and I am delighted with the book. There are four more very old-looking books, and a pile of paperback novels, but I'm not allowed to look through them all right now. I must look at the Sally Ann (Salvation Army) treasures she's brought for me to wear—two evening gowns, one of them complete with sequined bodice. I hold them up in front of me, eyebrows raised. I really can't see myself wearing either one. Jo insists I go and try them on, and Rick agrees with her. Under pressure from them both I go put the sequined one on. It fits me wonderfully, but it's a little too long. I can't quite get the zipper all the way up. I call Jo and hold my hair up while she zips it the rest of the way. We stand beside each other, looking in the full-length mirror. Jo has on stretchy denim jeans with a tucked-in shirt, turquoise and silver belt buckle ornamenting the front. She is maybe an inch taller than me and outweighs me by about thirty pounds. Those thirty pounds are placed strategically and I look small beside her. From a distance we could be an adolescent princess with her riper sister. We laugh, show Rick how gorgeous I am, and then I change back.

"Wear those dresses in the garden," Jo orders me.

"Okay." I humour her, knowing full well I'll never go out to the garden in either of the ball gowns. Jo tells me, "I mean it now. You should dress up as nice as you can at least once or twice a week. It makes you feel good. I put on fancy dresses and go for long walks whenever I can."

I try to picture her walking around South Hazelton in a fancy dress; I think she is probably getting a reputation as an eccentric there. I've only been through South Hazelton once and have a dim memory of it as a corner with a hotel. My memory doesn't furnish the town with any streets or houses, which Jo assures me do exist there.

She's brought a belt, a leather vest, and a sweatshirt for Rick. All of the clothing has a musty smell, likely from the second-hand store, and I throw it all in the laundry, even the gowns. She's brought a beaded house charm that she made; she gets me to hang it in the basement, out of the direct light, because she says it shows off best in reflected light. The house charm is a spiral wire hung with strings of beads. There are strings of plastic beads interspersed with strings of seed beads, and the plastic reflects the light in iridescent colour. Three prisms hanging at different levels complete the charm, and it is very pretty hung up.

"Charmed like how? Did you do a spell on it? Were you practising witchcraft, tying up your spells in beads?" I tease her.

"Never you mind, that could be true!" she laughs.

When seven thirty rolls around, and it's time for Rick and me to go to bed, Jo's ready too. She likes the room in the basement with the southeast window; it's ready and waiting for her. I get up at three a.m. with Rick when he goes to work, and I usually stay up. I try to be real quiet but soon after the log truck pulls out of the driveway, Jo comes upstairs.

"Good morning," she whispers.

"Same to you," I whisper back.

"Mmm...I smell coffee."

"Why are we whispering?"

"Doesn't seem right to talk out loud in the middle of the night." She's still whispering, and I start laughing. She does too—laughter is somewhat harder to whisper.

She gets her own coffee and sits at the table. I pour myself more and sit down across from her. She's got a funny look on her face, so I ask what's wrong.

"I'm scared, Janet, about seeing this specialist. What if he says its arthritis or something they don't know how to fix?"

"That's dumb, worrying about stuff like that before you even get there. It might just as easy be something they know exactly how to fix."

"It's not just that, I get panicky when I go into those big buildings. I'm always sure I'm going to do something wrong, get lost."

"End up in the operating room, on the table by accident, and they think you're the heart donor, and they take out your heart as you're trying to explain the mistake?"

"You're an ass," she tells me. "Will you come with me all the way? Like, not in the doctor's office, but in the waiting room?"

I laugh at her, but nod agreement. The temperature is ten below Celsius, perfect winter weather. It takes us an hour and a half to drive into Prince, and along the way she tells me about Maria's latest misadventure. Maria was on her way back to the camp job in her car when she was stopped by the RCMP and charged with failure to carry valid insurance; the cop let her go on the drinking, never even made her blow, although he warned her he could, and he tried to impress upon her the importance of not drinking and driving. As it was, they confiscated her car and she has a huge fine to pay that she can't afford. And she never made it back to the job.

"Did she just forget to renew it?"

"No, no, she just drove it; she never put insurance on it. Her old boyfriend bought it for her and he left insurance on it, but when it expired, at first she didn't notice, and then it was already a few months she'd been driving without, so she thought, 'What the hell, I'll just keep driving.' She didn't have insurance when we were here before. She's been driving it a long time already, and she figures she's saved half the price of the car already in insurance premiums."

"In all that time she never got stopped?"

"Nope, she never washed the car either, kept it real dirty."

Jo explains that Maria's insurance premiums are sky high because of stuff that happened in the past. "She'd never be able to afford insurance, so she opted out," Jo says. It strikes my funny bone. I didn't know that was an option. Jo goes on to tell me Maria has a new boyfriend in Terrace. She's moving in with him, and there's room for the kids too, the two youngest ones. She explains that the youngest is only eight, and she is acting up in school. They want her put on medication, and Maria is considering it. Jo tells me Maria's oldest kids are grown. One teenage boy is staying with his uncle; he's been there quite a while. Jo says they're smart kids, especially that one, he's doing real good.

"Have you met the boyfriend?"

"No. She just met him; she's been drinking quite a lot. No good can come of it." Jo shakes her head. "But the poor kids—they're not gonna be the winners either way."

Most of the drive we talk about Maria. We try to change the subject, but she keeps popping up. I visualize her kids; the youngest is the same age as one of my granddaughters, and somehow I super-impose her overtop and feel vaguely maternal towards these children who only exist for me in my imagination.

"I told her, 'Don't you friggin' dare let them put that sweet little girl on Ritalin or some other stupid drug. There's nothing wrong with that kid, she simply needs to get outside and run.' That's what all kids need," Jo fumes.

I agree. Too many kids are on drugs. I remember one of my own teachers, a very astute man who would make our grade six class drag our desks to the side every once in a while and make us do pushups, the whole class. He made it fun, giving out stars for performance and incidentally burning off that excess energy that had the more hyper children twitching in their seats. One of those hyper kids was me. Exercise is much more effective than drugs, and leaves the mind clear instead of foggy. If I saw him now I'd thank him for being such a great teacher. When I think of school I always think of him, how proud he'd be when we did well, how stern he was when we crossed him. Once I asked him if someone died when he first wore a new black suit, and I remember getting sent out into the hall to await my punishment. The agonizing wait in the corridor while I wondered if I was going to get the strap, the awful minutes wondering what was so bad about the question, and the relief when he finally appeared and gave me a talking to about rudeness and sent me back into the classroom. The punishment he let me give myself.

Finally, we seem to be able to leave Maria's life alone and we are on to other topics. Jo talks steadily as we get closer to the city.

Prince George isn't a big city; even with the new university the population is still under 100,000. We have to go to the Phoenix Medical Centre, and we easily find the right office and sit down to wait. It's taken Jo two and a half months to get in to see the specialist and her appointment is on time. She is gone fifteen minutes and then she's back. She picks up her coat that I've been holding, grabs my arm and squeezes it, looks at me full on, and flashes a very happy face. Then we put on our coats and retreat from the building in silence. The car is still warm from the drive in. Jo lets out a big breath and announces, "He can fix 'em, Janet. He can fix 'em." Then she bursts into tears, laughing at the same time. She takes off her glasses, wipes her eyes, and blows her nose. "Let's go to the dollar store," she says.

---

* Trying to fit in

Right from the day she arrived in the school, it seemed like Martha was marked as a troublemaker, which wasn't really the truth at all. Martha knew how to speak English; she was a very smart young girl and compassionate as well. At home she was very well behaved. She didn't know it, but the fact that she'd been kept at home till she was seven meant that her mother had somehow hidden her for the last three years. New policy at the school was to remove the children at a younger age. The previous students had mostly all reverted to their pagan ways as soon they were discharged from the schools, so the plan was to get them away from the bad influence of their parents' culture at an earlier age. Added to that was the policy of transferring payment from the government to the church on an enrollment headcount. The more children the better, but there was never enough money to run the schools properly even at that. To the matron of the school Martha seemed the embodiment of all that was wrong with the Native kids. There she was, too old to teach properly, with shells in her hair! The sight of the pagan girl's distress the first day when her hair was cut had given the matron a certain amount of satisfaction.

The first night Martha felt so lonely in the bed. She was used to sleeping with her mother, and when the small body of her cousin climbed in beside her she was happy for the contact. Snuggled together, they went to sleep. They woke suddenly, startled by the angry voice of the matron, shaking the smaller girl awake, and scolding loudly. "You're not puppies. Civilized people sleep alone, not in litters!" She grabbed Martha's cousin from the bed and propelled her towards her assigned bed on the opposite side of the room, emphasizing her words with a sharp slap on the behind.

Martha, startled by the slap, involuntarily said, "No—don't, don't…." The matron whirled and slapped her right across her cheek, snapping her head sideways and nearly knocking her over on the bed. Eight other wide-eyed dorm occupants stared in disbelief.

"Children do not talk back," the matron snarled at her, then stomped out of the dorm. The dorm supervisor, younger and softer looking than the matron, had been standing at stiff attention by the door till the woman left. Then she rushed over to Martha. "I'm so sorry. It's my fault," she said. "I saw it and let it go. I didn't know she'd come here this morning. I'm sorry. You all have to learn all the rules; one of the rules is you can't sleep together."

"She slapped me," Martha held her hand to the reddening cheek.

"She just used her hand, but she can do worse than that! You mind her, do what she says, stay out of trouble—out of her way," the kindly dorm supervisor advised.

Martha tried to stay out of trouble, but it didn't work. One of the first things that was taken away from the children was their language. They weren't allowed to speak their own language, only English. It would have been better for Martha if she hadn't known any English. As it was, she was used to translating, and when she attempted to translate what the teacher was saying to one of the uncomprehending children, she was not rewarded but punished. The teacher said, "Stand up, you—the one spouting that claptrap."

Martha stood. "Young lady, I advise you to cease speaking that vile tongue. In this school we will speak God's language, not that gobbledy-gook. You will go stand in the corner, with your back to the class." Martha stood still, not sure what to do. The teacher marched over, took her roughly by the shoulder, propelled her to the corner of the room, and pushed her face into the corner where she stood the rest of the morning, forehead leaning on the wall, wishing beyond hope for the comforts of home and the protection of her mother, vowing in her head to hate these people forever.

Martha was smart; it didn't take her long to figure out the rules. In the presence of the teachers and the clergy, Martha learned to be silent, only speaking when spoken to and acting very polite. When no adults were near enough to hear, she would make fun of the teachers, imitating them and making the other kids laugh. She had a gift for imitation and she did the long, sour face of the matron very well.

The schools were called industrial schools for a reason: the thought was to teach things that would prepare the children for jobs in the new world after their old way of life was destroyed. The schools taught agriculture, carpentry, shoemaking, blacksmithing, tinsmithing, and printing to the boys and cooking, cleaning, sewing, knitting, ironing, and dairying to the girls. The schools were segregated, boys on one side and girls the other. The children were not even allowed to speak to their male siblings. Martha knew she had a brother who was at the school, and every chance she got she studied the boys, wondering which one he might be. She wondered if she'd recognize him because she was only a baby when he was taken. He'd come home one summer, but she didn't remember. She knew his name was John.

Martha was always hungry at the school. At first, she hated the bare porridge they served for breakfast every day, but as she thinned down and her hunger grew, she looked forward to it. At home she'd never gone hungry; she could eat till she was full. At the school there was seldom enough food on the table for everyone to fill up. The children were served portions and not offered second helpings. It was different in the staff room: the butter that the children shook out of the cream ended up on the table there; there was buttermilk in the pitchers, toast with their breakfast, and sugar for their coffee. The rest of the milk was sold in town for the cash-strapped school. Though the children were used as free labour for the farm, their diet was not the healthy one that farm children usually enjoy; the farm produce was mostly sold to supplement the school's income.

There were parts of school that Martha liked: she liked singing, liked being outside in the gardens, and she liked the chickens and the animals. She hated doing dishes and cleaning the kitchen, didn't like the endless tubs of laundry or the endless buckets of potatoes to peel. She only liked cooking because sometimes she got extra to eat. Martha liked the dorm supervisor; she was the only adult who seemed as though she liked the children. This kind woman was the teacher for sewing and knitting. Martha enjoyed her class, sometimes she was funny and once she had everyone laughing out loud. The laughs died away suddenly when the matron appeared at the door and glared at the teacher, who was as quick to cast her eyes down as the children were. "No more of that ungodly racket," the matron ordered the suddenly subdued class.

Martha was a survivor; she learned to pocket food from the staff kitchen and eat it in hiding; she learned to be silent when her impulses were to laugh or scream or cry; she found a strength inside herself that kept her strong through the summer holidays and the winter ones, when some of the children could go home but she never could. One time it was because she "hadn't bowed her head in prayer," though she knew she had, and another time it was because she'd been skipping on Sunday. She knew she'd done that lots, but it was simply the first time she'd been caught. She still didn't get what was so bad about skipping, although she knew not bowing her head was a more serious issue: she could easily go to hell for that. Martha had to watch herself all the time so she didn't break any of God's rules. Martha knew there were many paths to hell and she tried hard to stay off them. She had no intention of going to the devil.

The butterfly

It took a long time for Jo to get in to see the specialist but not so long to actually get in for the surgery. At the appointment the doctor told her that he would scrape the tendons down so they would slide more smoothly and that would fix the problem. She only stayed to visit for five days in January since her next appointment was for February, so she'd be back soon.

While she was here in January, she was selling raffle tickets on a beaded butterfly hanger that she'd made. She described it as a butterfly-shaped hanger with strings of beads several feet long hanging from it, and more than 100 butterflies incorporated into it. The tickets were thirty bucks each, and both Rick and I had purchased them. She sold the last ticket and made the draw on the same day. She phoned me. "Guess what! Rick won the raffle!"

"That's awesome!"

"Friends of mine are going through and they're stopping at Newt's, so I'm gonna send it with them and you can pick it up there."

When I stop in to pick up the butterfly, Newt answers the door. He is starting to stoop when he walks, and he doesn't look very good—his complexion is grey, but his smile is genuine. "Janet, how good to see you." He gives me a hug and his woman, Sadie, gives me a hug as well. I used to like Sadie more before I found out why Jo left Newt. Now I keep a little reservation in the back of my mind for her. In fact, she and Newt both have rooms back there. For all the reservations I have, I still find them both charming, and I accept the coffee they offer me. We visit for a while, rehashing old times. Newt isn't doing much these days; he spends too much time in the local pub, and he smokes like a chimney while we visit. Their whole house stinks of cigarette smoke, and even though I smoke right now, I don't light one up in their house. I make another mental promise to myself to quit again. I hate the smell of cigarette smoke, in my hair and on my clothing, I don't know why I like it in my lungs. Back in the day when people smoked in bars and restaurants, the first thing I'd do when I got home was to wash my hair.

"Have you been to Jo's?" Newt asks.

"No. It's a trailer on a big lot, that's all she said."

"Us neither. One of these days me and Sadie are going to take a run up there," Newt says and Sadie nods. I don't know how Sadie feels about Newt's continuing friendship with Jo, but I have this feeling it isn't all peaches. She keeps trying to steer the conversation away from Jo, and Newt keeps grabbing the wheel and sliding it back.

Sadie is huge: she's always been big, but now she's beyond big. Jo tells me Sadie can't walk to the highway and back, a distance of less than an eighth of a mile. Neither one of them seems to have any ambition for cleaning up their yard; there is a shed with garbage bags spilling out the door, empty soft drink and booze bottles in a pile, fresh ones on top, older ones with their necks and sides glazed with snow. A rusty D8 Caterpillar crawler with the final drive out of it in pieces is sticking up through the snow, and beyond that is a row of rusting old cars. Piles of lumber and junk line the pathway to the house, and the path isn't shovelled, just a narrow packed trail to the door.

Each to their own, but I leave happy I'm not them. I don't open the garbage bag Jo packed her treasure in; I wait for Rick to get home. He pulls it out of the bag and holds it up while I untangle the strands. It's huge, and very beautiful. Rick shakes his head. "It says Jo all over it," is his verdict. We hang it upstairs above the balcony, glad we never put in the stained glass destined for that space. It twirls gently in the cross-currents of air up there near the peak and reflects light into hundreds of rainbow prisms on the wall. It's truly beautiful, and we're both pleased. We only bought the tickets so Jo would have some money to live on. I figure she made close to four hundred dollars with her raffle and she's so frugal that will probably last her all month.

I phone her the first week of February. There has been a warm Chinook wind blowing all day, and the temperature is a balmy plus four, unusual for winter in northern BC. Jo is not as happy about the melt as I am. "My friggin' roof is leaking. There is a huge spot in the living room, right beside where the cot is, water just drip, drip, dripping."

"Did you put a pot under it?"

"Of course, I did. What do ya think, I'm an idiot?"

"Uh..no. How come it's leaking?"

"It must have a hole."

"No kidding." Both of us start laughing. "What can you do about it?"

"That's the thing, I can't afford to do diddly-squat right now. I cut the ceiling board and pulled out all the insulation from where it's coming in. The insulation is all wet anyway, and it's no good when it's wet. I can't see any holes. I think I'm going to get a tarp and cover the whole roof."

"That's a good idea."

"The tarp costs forty-two dollars. I've got enough money to buy it, but then I don't have enough for the bus."

"I can get your bus ticket."

"Thanks."

Jo spends the rest of the week getting her place ready to leave. The tarp she finds for the roof is bright blue and will fit over the roof doubled up, but first she has to get the rest of the snow off. She has to be real careful because the roof is pretty soft in places. She can see the roof ribs—the roofing dips between them—and she has to make sure to only stand on them. She figures out a method of shovelling that puts a minimal strain on the hands, pushing the weight with her shoulders and using her wrists as guides. At the edge of the roof, she only has to turn the shovel instead of lifting. It's sometimes easier to do things than to think about doing them. For Jo, this isn't one of those times; doing it is slow, tedious going and she's just begun when the preacher shows up. He found out via the "moccasin telegraph" that she was up on her roof and asks if he can help. Normally she doesn't like asking for help—she doesn't like feeling indebted, but she house-sat his place this spring and knows him well enough to accept. Gratefully. Between the two of them it still takes the whole day to get the roof shovelled and the tarp on. She bought a big one on sale for the same price as the smaller one. "Double my pleasure," she said to the clerk when she bought it. They try to tie the grommets to shrubs and the picnic table, to the steel stove in the yard, to anything heavy or anchored in the earth, but the folded side doesn't have any grommets and despite their best efforts it keeps flapping in the wind. Jo has the brainwave to put something heavy right on the tarp to hold it down and mentally catalogues her supply of heavy things that she can still lift and settles on tires. She has a pile of tires in the backyard, which she'd meant to use as potato planters, but now they seem like the solution to her problem. They dig them out of the snow and the preacher helps her wrestle the ladder around the trailer and he does the climbing, each time carrying a tire and placing it atop the blue tarp. By the time they're finished, eight tires and a blue tarp provide a drip-free roof that hardly flaps at all.

Jo decides it's safest if she gets the town to shut off the water, then if the place freezes, well, no big deal. The worker turns the valve at the edge of the lot and tells her when she gets back to give them a call for reconnection, and just so she knows, there will be a charge for the service of reconnecting the water. It seems like every time she turns around someone wants more money! "How much?"

"Thirty-five dollars."

"Thirty-five dollars to come and turn a valve?"

The woman nods. Jo had watched the operation as they turned the water off, and she vows to herself she'll not ask the next time. She is quite capable of turning the valve. Still, it's better the water is turned off because if a line in the trailer breaks when she isn't home for a few months, then it would be the end of it. When she turns the key and puts it in its hidey hole at the end of the week she's pretty sure everything will be good for the few months she'll be gone.

There are different levels of trust built into people. Babies simply trust everyone; distrust comes later, once we begin to focus on polarity, the good and bad, the hot and cold of it. It's a physics law that every action has to have an equal and opposite reaction; the average level of distrust seems to be born in reaction, and if it was a ladder most of us would be clinging to the lowest rung. Jo and her brother learned very young that people are basically untrustworthy. Their dad and uncle, so caring and loving when sober, could forget to care for the kids when they were drinking; they could leave the kids in the back seat of the car outside the hotel, and they could be gone when they needed protection. Jo and Sam learned to look after themselves during these times. In the summer they knew where the berries grew, and in the winter they knew how to open a jar of salmon or eat a pocket full of dried apples. They learned what doors were open to small children any time, and they learned what doors would never open for them. Jo still gets tears in her eyes when she tells of a street where no one would answer their door even when a frightened little girl came knocking. The kids learned to hide when the parties got rowdy.

While Jo and Sam were still very young, their dad and uncle left the logging camp and moved close to Telkwa, a small town east of Smithers on the Bulkley river, and the men did lots of work around the area. They knew many different trades, and Jo thinks they were good carpenters. A specialty of theirs was stucco finishing for homes, grinding their own glass to make the top coating. They were skilled artisans who supplemented their income by bootlegging. In Jo's memory, they were cheerful, careful workers who took great pride in their work. Another equally clear memory has her peeking out the bedroom window while a cop car comes to the door to buy a bottle.

The kids weren't supposed to look out the windows after dark. "Keep the curtains closed!" was a rule, but one the kids broke a lot.

Jo was very shy when she was young, (she's still shy now), and she remembers peeking at strangers from the safety of her father's presence, her arm firmly wrapped around his leg. "Don't know how he could walk—me hanging on his leg like that." When he wasn't drinking heavily, he looked after the kids, taking pride in them, hauling them to church on Sundays, and enrolling them in public school. He always braided Jo's hair every morning, and she still likes to have her hair braided the way he did it. He took them to the Mormon church; Jo wasn't very old when she heard and understood the minister preaching the sermon about how the people of the earth with dark skins were not going to the same heaven as the white skins. Jo quizzed her dad about it on the way home. "What did he mean, Dad? Me and Sam have dark skin, and you don't. Are we going to your heaven?" To his credit, her dad answered that the preacher did mean that, and that the preacher believed that it was true, which didn't necessarily make it so. Jo told him that she didn't like that preacher and she didn't want to go to his church anymore, and again, to his credit, her dad didn't force the issue. Since that day, Jo has spurned organized religion. She believes in a creator, not a God. "There's a difference," she says. "A creator makes things and then loves them; if he doesn't, then he fixes them. They're his artwork, his life. If there's something wrong with his creations, then it's his fault, not theirs. You can't blame the picture if you painted it wrong. The real creator fixes things: she's inside us; she's that urge to do things right, to create beauty; she's Mother Nature and all of that. The creator wants us to do good, to flourish. That God, on the other hand, seems a little bit petty and more than a little bit mean. Too much testosterone! He supposedly made everything; the earth, us, everything. Then, because we're not perfect, we're going to hell? If he made everything, then he must've made hell! Where's the responsibility—with us that's flawed? Or with that God? You think there's only one God, the one that white people found? Surely other peoples could at least have their own God, their own champion!"

Jo and Sam were the only Native kids in the public school. Their dad made them go. All the other Native kids were in the residential school, no longer as residents unless they were orphans or lived far away, but as bused-in students. The German Mormon wasn't having his kids in any church-run school, so off they went to public school. From the moment they got to school they found they were the objects of attention, not much of it the kind of attention a young kid craves.

Jo learned young what discrimination is; at school in the early sixties, the general public saw the Natives as lesser people. Some still do: they'll point at the drinkers hanging out in town as though they are the representatives of their race, as though Vancouver's Lower East Side is representative of Vancouver. Some people say that before white men came the Natives were starving to death and living in dirty hovels, but now they have electricity and nice homes and nice cars and lots of food and they don't need to do anything because the government sends them a cheque every month. They honestly think that the colonizing nations made the lives of the Native population better. It's an attitude failure, a reality check that hasn't been completed. The measurement is skewed—measuring material gain only. In that respect they are partially correct: material gains have made daily living easier right across society, and hardly anyone would like to go back to hauling water and using the outhouse in twenty below weather, although people who did that were seldom obese.

What's not so easy to see is another's emotional and cultural security, the confidence we take for granted in the correctness of our own basic beliefs. For Natives, this has been systematically eroded through hundreds of years of overt discrimination, the general public believing they were superior to Natives. After all, they reasoned, Natives were "primitive," "lazy," and "savage," not "civilized" at all. Worldwide, the colonizers failed to see the underlying values and worldviews of the societies they so superciliously robbed and overthrew. Jo and Sam's classmates couldn't help but have their attitudes: the worldview of the parents is visited on the children unbidden. That's why the government removed the Native children from the care of their parents in the first place, so the children might instead absorb the colonial worldview. Big favour, that!

Jo is so sensitive to being looked down upon; she sometimes sees it where I swear it doesn't exist. We'll have disagreements as to whether this person or that is racist; she claims she can see it in their eyes. She remembers the first time she was fully aware of that look.

Jo was around five or six years old, and not going to school yet, when she and Sam were helping their dad and uncle with the glass spraying on a house in Smithers. The bottom line around the house was from the green bottles that they'd helped gather and grind. It was cold and the kids were keeping warm around the little fire Dad made in the yard. Uncle had promised all afternoon that when they were done they'd stop at the restaurant in Smithers and get a hot chocolate. When they got to the restaurant, the waitress came to the table. She had on a white skirt and a blue shirt, and her hair was pulled up off her face with a white bow on the side of it. At first, Jo thought she looked pretty, but then she looked directly at her and her eyes weren't pretty, they were hard and mean. She sniffed at Sam and Jo, actually sniffed like they didn't smell good. She told the men that she would serve them but not the children—they didn't serve Indians. Jo's dad and uncle sat there silent, and each of them smoked a whole cigarette. When they butted out, they all left, and no one had anything. The hurt from that encounter is still in Jo's voice decades later, when she can go anywhere and get a hot chocolate.

"You can sometimes tell by looking at people what kind of person they are. Some of them have those mean eyes. Some walk around with their lips all pursed up like they just sucked on a lemon, and you know that person is going to criticize everything and everybody." Jo stretches out her nose and puckers up a sour face. "Or if they have their shoulders all rounded down, you know the weight of the world is on them, and that person is gonna be cranky or sad. But sometimes you can't tell: someone might appear to be one thing and be something else entirely."

"Like what?"

"Like someone might appear to be your friend, when in fact it's someone who wants to use you. Those kind of people, they can use you right up."

"Eventually they show their hand, though, don't you think? No one can hide their true nature all the time," I observe.

"Funny you should say that," Jo says. "That's what I am beginning to be able to sense. I can sense phoniness, and I can sense bad energy. Like when I was out in the garden in the summer, I had on a nice sundress and I was watering the garden with the hose, and all of a sudden I felt cold even though the sun was shining and it was hot. I glanced around and saw a man standing in the street staring in; it made me shudder. I knew he was dangerous; there was a blackness coming out of him, and I pretended I didn't see, turned off the hose and went around to the back door and went inside. I watched him out the window where he couldn't see me and he waited a while and then walked away. I think he must have been the rapist: the neighbour said there was a rapist living around here. I keep my gate shut, and that day I locked my house too."

---

*Lost

Martha's self-preservation instinct served her well for her first years at the Indian Industrial Residential School. The dorm supervisor was kind and sided with the children, but she interfered with the matron once too often over discipline. The young woman had been "let go," a polite euphemism for the firing of the child-friendly teacher. The matron was a firm believer in "spare the rod and spoil the child." It was a common belief at the time; it came with the colonizing people, a belief that many still cling to. This belief can be exercised in a number of ways, from the disciplinarian who needs only to give the child one smack on the rear as a toddler to inflict a life-long understanding of consequence, right to the other end of the scale where the parent feels obliged to beat the children daily, "for the children's own good."

It was a belief that the Native populations did not endorse. They raised their children without corporal punishment and would have disrespected anyone who would raise a hand to a child. Modern beliefs in Canada have gone this route, and it is now against the law to spank children. A person who spanks their child can be reported to the authorities and the children removed from the care of the spanker. But at the time, being victims of the prevailing beliefs, Martha and her schoolmates were subjected to beatings for both minor and major offences. Beatings varied in intensity, the strap being the most commonly used method of applying the rod. The offending student would be called to the front of the room and would hold out their hand while the teacher administered blows to the palm with a wooden paddle.

There were proscribed numbers of blows for each of the different offences. The rest of the class had to watch: if they employed their custom of not seeing by casting the eyes down, the teachers could and would make it worse. Sometimes the matron made one of the other students do the hitting. She was the worst of all—the meanest teacher there and uniformly hated by all but a few students. These were called her pets and could do no wrong in her eyes. They became her ears and her eyes in the dorms, and many a child was beaten on the strength of stories carried back to her.

Martha had perfected her imitation of the matron and one day she performed it in the kitchen, stretching her round face out and down into the long, sour face, lips pursed while she pretended to scold her classmates in the matron's accents for the dirty dishes. She had just finished saying "Cleanliness is next to Godliness" when the stilled faces of her audience warned her of her danger. It was too late to do anything about it, so she turned and faced the matron herself. The woman's eyes were glinting with the promise of vengeance. The matron reached out and grabbed her by the sleeve, marched her to the confinement room, thrust her inside, and locked the door.

It was the first time Martha had been to The Room, but it wasn't the first she knew of it. The big girls were usually kept in there when they were bad, and Martha had heard crying and screaming coming through the door at various times. There was a conspiracy of silence about it: everyone pretended not to know anything about it, but everyone did. The very sight of the door always gave Martha the creeps, and being thrown inside totally freaked her out. The key turning in the lock sounded like a gunshot. The room contained a cot and a chair, nothing else. Martha crouched down, her back to the door and dread in the pit of her stomach.

"Please God, if you're real, please look after me" she prayed.

When Jo arrives on the bus she once again has her bags packed to the limit. She's been shopping at the Sally Ann, and once again she brings clothes for Rick and me. This time she gives me a leather jacket, suede with fringes at the hem and across the back. It fits me perfectly and I love it. I put it on with my brown bib overalls and a western hat, and now I look like I just stepped out of a Louis L'Amour novel.

She's brought a beaded curtain, done in the same style as the butterfly hanger, and tells me she wants to sell it and wonders how much she might get.

There are a lot of factors governing the price of objects, labour being only one. I know each string of beads takes time, and there are hundreds of strings on the curtain. If it was done in a third world country and bought by a western buyer, it might sell in a store for a couple of hundred dollars. But this is Canada where we expect to make upwards of ten dollars an hour for the most menial work. On the other hand, this is art and in Canada artists don't get much pay or recognition, so we don't value our work for the true cost of our labour, let alone the materials.

"I don't want to buy it and sell it too," I tell her. "You tell me what you think it's worth and I'll buy it from you. It's beautiful and I love it."

"I was thinking about five hundred for it, but if you want it I'll give it to you for four."

"Done!" I say. "I'll get some money out when we go to town."

"Whenever," she replies.

The surgery is set for Wednesday, but she has to go into outpatients in Vanderhoof and have blood work done on Tuesday. She's not supposed to eat or drink anything after supper or in the morning, then she goes back for day surgery Wednesday morning. Jo explains that she will be put out for the operation, but when she wakes up she'll be able to come home. I take her into Vanderhoof hospital, and go right into the room with her and stay while they get her ready, in case she's scared. I don't like hospitals myself, and I've been known to faint visiting inpatients; the atmosphere sometimes overwhelms me. I am happy when the nurse who shows up to prepare Jo is someone I know. Sherry's been a nurse for years, and I know Jo is in good hands. We chat and Jo relaxes. "You can go now," she says and dismisses me with a wave.

"See you on the other side," I say, and Sherry tells me to come back around eleven thirty, that Jo will be done around then. I go downtown, buy groceries, fill up the car, go to the bank, and do everything on the town list, but it's still only ten thirty. I buy a book and sit in the waiting room. I'm there when Sherry comes looking.

She smiles and tells me Jo will be right along. "Everything went very well," she says. "Is she staying with you? I notice she's from Hazelton."

"Yeah, until her hand gets better enough to function again," I say.

"Good, she'll need some help with the basics for a few days till things start to heal."

Sherry smiles and hands over a prescription for pain medication that I can have filled at the drugstore before we leave town. She tells Jo it was nice to meet her and that she hopes she'll heal quickly. We need to make an appointment at the clinic to have the stitches removed in about a week.

Jo says to head for home when we get in the car; she doesn't need the pain medication. It hardly hurts at all, and she doesn't like to take medication. I go along with her and we drive straight home. Her hand is completely bandaged, just the tips of her fingers showing. She holds it in front of her and seems pretty spaced out. "I was scared about the anesthetic," she confides in a sleepy voice. "I was worried it would be like a seizure when you lose consciousness, but it wasn't like that at all. He told me to count backwards from one thousand, and that confused me well enough. I think I only got two numbers out and I don't remember anything till I woke up in the recovery room."

When we get home Jo goes straight to bed, and sleeps through supper. Rick and I are very quiet so we don't disturb her. We go to bed early, even for us. I wake up around eleven, not sure what woke me up at first. I finally decide it's Jo; she's making whimpery noises and sounds like she's in the living room below us. I slide into a housecoat and go down to see what's wrong.

She's sitting on the couch with her eyes closed, rocking gently back and forth with her hand cradled up to her chest. Tears are running down her cheeks and she is very quietly moaning. "Jo, what's wrong?" She hears me and opens her eyes. "Holy God, Janet, my hand hurts so much, I can't stand it."

"I have some 292s here: will you take a couple? Did you eat anything yet?"

"I wish I'd have listened and got the bloody painkillers they offered me."

"Why didn't you?"

"They cost a lot, and I'm flat-ass broke. I can't afford pain pills."

"That's ridiculous. I owe you for the curtain, and I have your money. Anyway, I'll get those 292s, but you'd better eat something first, so you don't puke them up. Toast?"

Jo eats two pieces of toast and jam, and washes it down with juice and pain pills. I stay up with her for the next half hour till they kick in and she assures me the pain's tamed down to bearable.

In the morning, I run into town and get Jo's prescription filled. She took the last 292 we had when she got up. She says it's throbbing, and before I go we rig up a support that lets her keep it elevated above her shoulder. It seems to hurt less when it's up high.

I am a crappy nurse. I can't clean up puke without sympathy puking, and I tend to give the sympathy taught by my dad, things like: "long way from your heart," and "you'll live; you're tough." I don't like the sight of the wound in her hand when we change the dressing, so I don't look, and I'm glad when she tells me it's looking better after a couple of days. She starts doing stuff and trying to bend her fingers, but then it starts hurting again. She takes medication, feels better, and then overdoes it again. She quits taking the pain medication. "It doesn't hurt that much now, and if I take the pills I can't tell when I'm overdoing it. Pain is telling you to stop doing what you're doing, and the pills are masking that. They were good when it was bad, but I think it'll be better if I don't take the rest of these. Put 'em in your medicine cabinet."

When we go get the stitches out there is a sudden, marked improvement. Jo says, "It went 'ping' when that middle stitch came out, and look how they bend now." She's right: she can curl all her fingers into a fist, and she's wearing a grin that lights up the car.

Devil comes calling

Jo being shy didn't help her in school, but Sam was always there, at recess and lunch hour, and it didn't matter to him if the other boys teased him about being a sissy hanging out with a girl.

"Come on, Sister. Come and play with me," he'd say, and he was tough enough to defend himself and her from the ones who'd want to bully them. He failed a grade, so they were in the same class. Jo learned to read and write, something she loved to do. Her writing grew perfect, and she treated it like art, the strokes carefully practised in line after line of neat handwriting. When she learned to sound out the alphabet she read everything, and soon she could read anything. Her desire to know about things made reading easy.

The first years of school made Jo feel the absence of her mother acutely. Everyone else had a mother, everyone in their whole class. Before that time she'd taken it for granted that she didn't have a mother and wasn't even sure what position a mother would have taken in their home. She knew other kids had mothers; she used to daydream about holding hands with her mother who had come to pick her up from the school. Her mother would hold out her hand and Jo would take it; she and Sam would hold their mother's hands and walk down the street just like other kids. She was beginning to know they weren't like other kids, though. She bugged her dad so much about her mother that he decided to take her to her grandmother. Martha was living in a small house by herself on the edge of town; Jo was surprised to see that she was Indian. She had a lot of interesting things in her home: jars on the shelf full of who knows what and pretty things from the beach. There were pieces of driftwood polished by the waves and the sand into shiny ebony, and elaborate sea shells that you could hear the ocean in. They walked the seashore and picked up seaweed and clams that her grandmother cooked, and she had a boat that she took Jo out in to catch fish from the ocean. Jo remembers the smell of the ocean, the heat of the cookstove, and the warmth of her grandma's lap. She remembers the old woman bent over her needlework at the kitchen table, her long braid undone and her hair, mostly black still, spread in ripples over her shoulder. She remembers the security she felt there. Still, she was glad when her dad came to get her because she missed him and Sam so much.

Jo's dad used to worry about the lack of feminine influences in her life. There was no one to teach her how to wear shoes and dress pretty, how to set the table right, all those things that women unknowingly teach. To see that Jo got these kinds of lessons, he occasionally took her to stay in the summer with an older couple, friends from the church. They had a farm and their own children were grown. Jo loved staying on the farm. She didn't like all the bathing and all the fussing about clothes, but it was worth putting up with so she could play on the farm. She loved getting the eggs and throwing the grain out for the chickens to peck; she loved the farmyard with its assortment of critters; she loved the kittens in the barn who would come close only when fresh milk was served; and she found an attachment for farm life that stuck with her. But, at the end of her summer stays, the most welcome sight in the world was her dad's vehicle rolling into the yard.

Little did she know that her security was soon to be taken away for good. Jo's dad and uncle were drinkers, but they were also there for the children all the time. Until the day they weren't. The man who shattered their lives became the man Jo hated most in the whole world. Chester was a cruel and vicious person, disguised in the body of a nice-looking man with a gracious company face. He made friends easily, and his true face only came out after he knew a person and had probed their weaknesses. Then he abused with violence and sex. Almost everyone was afraid of him. Jo believes even the cops were scared of him, and that's why he was able to hurt so many people. Jo thinks her dad didn't know that his "friend" was also a child rapist who targeted her as a victim when she was about eight. Her dad was a Mormon preacher's son, and sexual predators didn't show up on his radar. She has no idea where her father was when it happened, and to this day she doesn't know. Neither does her brother. All she knows is she woke up from a dead sleep with Chester's large hand over her mouth. He pulled her by the head to the edge of the bed, leaned down and whispered in her ear. "Make a noise or tell anyone, and I'll kill your brother." A full-grown man, having his way with an eight-year-old child. Jo's brother slept on beside them till Jo made an involuntary noise and woke him. When he realized what was going on, Sam leaped up and tackled the offender as well as a ten-year-old boy could. He was felled with a vicious blow to the head, and Chester departed. He left behind two traumatized children, both suffering from assault, one bleeding from a four-inch gash in his skull. They both felt guilty: him for not protecting her and her for waking him. Neither reported the incident to their father.

"He might have tried to stop him, but where was he? Where was he that night? I couldn't take the chance Chester would kill Sam."

Jo can't remember without breaking down and crying. "He was already bleeding so much I was scared he was going to die. All I could do was wrap my pillowcase around his head for a bandage. He got stitches in his head later that night. I think Uncle came and took him to the hospital. I think he said it happened by falling on a lamp shade, but I don't know how that lie got started." I hope she's crying away some of the trauma; I hope it works like that. I'm sorry I'm making her remember painful things, but she says it's okay. "Anyway, it wasn't long after that I got taken away and put into foster care."

"How come? Did someone at the school figure it out?"

"Again, I don't know. What I do know is that I came to school with a black eye. I can't remember how I got it, and my brother doesn't remember either. The teacher and the principal talked to me, but I don't even know what I said. I never got to go home. They took me to stay with this big Dutch woman. When I got there she fed me up. I never in my life had to eat so much food, and after supper she told me to go get my pajamas on and get ready for bed. I told her I wasn't tired and she stomped her foot. I can still see her standing there in her dress and apron, her hands on her hips. She didn't say nothing, just gave her foot that stomp on the floor, but I tell you, by God, I raced in there and got those PJs on and got in bed, even though I wasn't a bit sleepy. At home we pretty well stayed up till we were tired."

"Did Sam come too?"

"No, that's another story. For some reason they didn't take Sam away." Her face darkens. "They should have! Or maybe not—who knows?"

"What happened to him?"

"After they took me away, Dad moved to Prince Rupert. Actually, he was working for a guy who had a huge warehouse, and he let Dad build a little room inside the warehouse. He put a little heater in it, and that's where him and Sam lived while I was in foster homes. It seems to me like he was hiding there, but Sam went to school till he was in grade eight, so he must have put him in school. I didn't see him again till I was fourteen, and I couldn't hardly believe it was Sam. I hadn't seen him for almost six years. He was so handsome, and I loved him so much it almost hurt."

"Was the Dutch lady mean?"

"No. She was really nice. They had a farm and lots of animals. They did the same things every day: there were cows to milk, and they made their own butter and cheese. I wasn't there for more than a few days before I was wearing new dresses that she had made for me."

"How long did you stay there?"

"I don't know. My memories are all jumbled up, and I don't know when lots of things happened. I remember some things very clearly, just not when. I can't even say how many foster homes I lived in. Some were nice, some not so nice, and some downright abusive. None of them were home, because none of them had my dad or my brother. I missed my brother; it was always me and Sam before. I think I missed Sam most of all. Later I found out he carried on a campaign of his own: one time he busted the windshield out of the bastard's car, and another time he slashed the tires."

"I don't get where your father was in all of this?"

"Me neither, Janet. Where was my father?"

"You told me that man got charged. Did he go to jail?"

"That was a long time after. Lots of time, lots more hurting he done.

His own kids charged him. First only one, and then because she was going to court alone and no one else would say, her sister stood up and said she was telling the truth, that it happened to her too. At least thirty years that man was having sex with children, and some of them women knew. Some of those children grew up.

"I'll tell you what I saw him do when I was a little girl. I don't know why we were there, but I remember the house was made with a stairway that you could see from down below. Chester was mad about something. His wife was a tiny little woman, real pretty. He was yelling at her and hitting her. They were at the top of the stairs, and he pushed her down. She went all the way down and while she was falling he jumped over her, and when she got to the bottom he kicked her. That's how he was, so mean that everyone was scared of him—his family, the cops, everyone. He was a violent, angry, horrible person, and until you knew him you'd never figure that. He always seemed okay at first impression; people liked him and he made friends easy, but that was always short lived. He just figured out how he could use people and then he did."

"If other people knew, why wouldn't they have said?"

"I thought about that lots, and you know what I think? They were so afraid. I just can't tell you how afraid, until you been there you don't have no reference point. I think as long as he was bothering us, he wasn't bothering them. I think there was a few more knew and didn't want to believe it. He was like a bad stain that wouldn't stop spreading."

"That's really ugly."

"Ain't nothing pretty about any of it." Jo's eyes get hard and brittle as she takes this memory walk, and once more I feel like I'm intruding.

"What happened to him after he got out of jail? Did he move to some other place and carry on?"

"Hell, no. He moved back home."

"Back to his wife? After she knew he raped their children?"

Her voice goes real quiet. "It was Maria's dad—she's the one who stood up when her sister accused him and said she was telling the truth. He's dead now, and I have to say I'm glad. I hated him like

I hated no one else. I actually haven't hated anyone else in my whole life; there was no room for anyone else in my hate."

"How did you ever become friends with Maria?"

"I met her when I was visiting back home, years ago. She was the waitress, and she was so friendly and nice I liked her right away. We were instant friends. When I found out her last name I almost cried."

"It's good you got away from him," I say.

She looks at me like I have rocks in my head. "My father got me back when I was a teenager. He quit drinking and got me back. We went to court, and in the middle of all that, Dad stood up in court and he said, 'Who do you love, Jo?' The judge was saying, 'You're out of order; you're out of order,' but I answered him, 'I love you, Dad.' And at the end of it all I got to go home," her voice saddens. "But he was an alcoholic, and he never could stay sober for long."

Jo is a frugal person. It's something she takes pride in, but no one can live on nothing. She's done a lot of jobs, but they all involve physical labour and none are jobs she can do now. Her hand is getting better; she curls it into a fist to show how great it's working. It bends very nicely and has the strength of a six-year-old's—maybe not quite. As soon as she gets it strong enough to use she has to go get the same thing done to the other hand. I don't see how she's going to live. I worry about it.

"I got a plan," she says. "I'm putting my name out as house-sitter. I can look after pets and stuff while people are vacationing or going away for any reason. It's easy, and I figure I can ask fifty dollars a day and get it."

She might be able to get it. It would add seven hundred dollars to the cost of a two-week vacation, but it costs quite a bit to put dogs and cats in kennels, so maybe it's a good idea. "Got any takers yet?"

"Yeah, I've got two lined up already. I'm going to Walkers' end of March, and then I'm staying at Newt and Sadie's for a couple days, then the next two weeks at some other friends'."

"What about your place? Is it okay to leave it? And what about your house payments?" Jo is buying her place privately from the previous owner. She's paying him direct: no lawyer, no realtor.

"He's not in a big rush to get paid. He still holds the title, and he's gonna sign it over when I finish paying him. I still owe two thousand, but he'll wait."

"You don't have title?"

"Not yet, not till I finish paying him."

"Is he a good guy? You can trust him?"

"No, he isn't what you'd call a good guy—he's a wicked old shyster, but I believe he'll be fair to me. He was a friend of my dad's, and I'm a friend of his daughter's, and I helped her out a lot. He remembers those things."

That doesn't sound too reassuring to me. It seems like the winds of chance have to blow very carefully, so they don't blow Jo away. There should be some social network for Jo to fall back on. She's Nisga'a: they're getting self-government, and in my opinion, the first thing a good government does is to take care of its citizens. I think that the Nisga'a nation gets transfer monies based on the numbers of their citizens, and the band has been getting money from the day Jo was born simply because she exists. And yet, she never gets anything from them, so it seems to me that Jo needs to get after the Nisga'a for support till she's functional again.

"No," she says, "I tried that. My friend Pam went up there with me. Nisga'as will only do something if I go live on reserve. Big fat chance of me doing that. I wouldn't live there if they paid me a bundle. You think politics are bad out here, you should see what it's like on a reserve. Every two years they pit family against family for elections, and then they wonder why everyone doesn't get along."

"What about welfare?"

"I'm not broke enough to go on welfare. I haven't been on welfare my entire life, and I'm not about to start now. I'm surprised you'd say that. Do you think I've sunk quite that low, that I'll turn into a welfare bum?"

Jo's in a huff, but I didn't mean to make her mad. "Just a suggestion."

"A poor one. Social services would always be snooping in my life, telling me how I can live. Those people think they own you, and you always have to go and beg for your money. I know lots of people on welfare, most of them because they're lazy. I wouldn't even qualify, because I have a house. They wouldn't let me keep my house. They'd say I don't qualify."

"Okay, but Jo, that's a social net that's supposed to keep people from crashing. There has to be something for people when they get into your circumstances. What about disability?"

"What's disability?"

"It's from the government, sort of a pension for when you're not able to work. There's short-term and long-term."

"That's exactly me. I'm short-term disabled. How do you get that?"

I have no idea how a person gets on disability, I tell her to ask the doctor; she still has to go one more time for follow-up. She comes home with a bunch of papers from the doctor and some forms we stop at the access centre to get. The doctor actually phoned the provincial access centre and told the lady there what forms Jo needs.

She still has trouble picking up a coffee cup, so she starts exercising the hand more every day. She takes a rubber ball and squeezes it, counting the numbers of squeezes and increasing daily. She suffers for it in the evenings but won't take painkillers. Jo decides not to have the other hand done till next winter. She says she has to be able to use her hands in the summer, and the worst one is fixed already. It's good enough to use—a hell of a lot better than it was last year—and she's just begun to get the yard looking the way she wants it. Added to all that is the worry of the anesthetic. Last time the after-effects left her feeling weaker, more prone to blackouts. She feels good about making that decision.

Jo loves to garden. She has a double lot in town, and the trailer has a pretty small footprint, so there is lots of room to grow things. The climate is nicer in Hazelton than in central BC, meaning that it's warmer. The pine and spruce forest begins to give way to cedar along the highway, and plants that winterkill further inland will live. Jo reads everything in the house about intensive gardening, and she intends to grow as many things as she possibly can. She is well versed in herbal lore, and we are both amazed that people used to store all that information in their heads. Jo laughs. "I don't think my head is big enough to store all that!" She is very interested in healthy eating and local growing, subjects dear to my heart. It's nice to have someone to talk to who shares your interests, a kindred spirit, and the time goes by quickly. Soon it's time for her to go house-sitting, and I'm sorry to see her go. Having her here is like having a grown-up, live-in, sister.

We're so sorry

I'm researching the residential schools, and I know that the Canadian government has issued a formal apology. I go hunting around on the net to find out who said what. Prime Minister Stephen Harper delivered Canada's apology on June 11, 2008. He apologized for the schools and said the burden of the schools belongs to the government and the country. He said we now recognize how profoundly we hurt the Natives by public policy and committed the government to work towards forging a new relationship between aboriginal peoples and other Canadians, based on knowledge of history, respect, and desire.

It seems to me to be too little, too late. If we really are going to change, to base our relationship on history and respect, the government will have to add the values of aboriginal peoples into the equation when talking about resources and developments like pipelines.

I have a book called *Touch the Earth*, subtitled *A Self-Portrait of Indian Existence*, compiled by T.C. McLuhan, published in 1971, that has 170 pages of Native North American wisdom given during the last four hundred years. Most of the words have been transcribed from government documents. Often the words are given in despair, when the governments have taken away the Natives' rights to pretty well everything. Many of them plead not for themselves but for the earth. They say that the earth is alive and that we must treat it with respect. The environmental degradation that we are experiencing today was clearly foretold by these wise men and women.

I wish I could go back and tell them their visions have not come true, but all too often I look around and see that they have.

Will parliament ever sit around and discuss what effects a policy might have on the people of the future? Will MPs look past their billfolds, peer seven generations ahead, and see what impacts the decisions they make today might have on those people? So far it seems not: actions speak louder than words. What will happen to the people when our resources are stripped away, when there is no easy oil to pump, no difficult oil to extract, no gold left to be found? Stripped mountains, oil spilled in pristine waters, wild game with cancers, poisoned water and air: the tears of the visionaries have foretold them all.

They say, "The earth is alive." It's not an inert object conveniently spinning about for us to exploit; it's a living organism that we in turn depend on for our lives.

The prime minister has committed the government to a new relationship based on knowledge, respect, and desire. The truth about the residential school experience is before the public eye, the government convened a panel called the Truth and Reconciliation Commission to look into the wrongdoing. Anyone who cares to can look up stories on the Internet. Pick almost any residential school and you'll find horrendous stories. For victims of these schools that apology from the prime minister of Canada means a lot—the government apology means recognition of the wrong perpetrated by the very existence of the schools. Government represents us, the people, all of us.

It's hard to define "respect" and "desire," almost as hard as it is to define "knowledge." Some Native knowledge is written, although traditionally the knowledge was handed down orally, yet all agree the earth is alive. Given that knowledge, do we choose to believe?

The question remains to be answered about what the new relationship will look like between Canada's government and the Native inhabitants, all of us Canadians.

---

* Martha begets Sarah

When Martha finally returned home she'd been gone for five years. She had left at seven years old and returned at twelve. She couldn't help but notice how small and untidy everything was. Her mother had a new baby boy, named John. Her mother believed that he was her brother who had died at the school, born again as the new baby. Martha wondered if she should tell her mother that God was keeping the dead people, but decided against it. Her mother wasn't like she remembered and neither was her father. They were a lot smaller, and it was hard to speak to her father at all. He didn't know English, and she had to reach so far to recall his language. It was easier to speak English with her mother and have her tell her father what she said.

At the school Martha always finished her prayers with a silent request to be returned home to her family. Now that her prayers were answered, she thought she should be grateful, but it really felt like an anticlimax. Things didn't seem right. Gone was the feeling of security that she associated with home; she no longer felt comfortable there. She felt so much shame for her family: they did things that were savage and uncivilized. When the baby got sick and the medicine men showed up with their masks and shakers she wanted to hide, to tell her parents that they were from the devil. She wanted them to get the white doctor from the store and for them all to pray. When the baby recovered she knew it was because God had answered her own prayers.

It took weeks, then months for Martha to get used to the freedom. She felt like she was in a world where she didn't fit anymore. She was closer to the friends she'd gone to school with than she was with her own family. She started hanging out with a group from the school. They were reinventing themselves in a society they no longer fit into.

Martha married when she was sixteen to a boy who had gone to a different school. He would never talk about school, and he didn't believe in God, but he was funny and kind. He liked traditional things and he liked to drink as well. Martha started drinking with him, and it wasn't long till they had a noisy bunch of toddlers and a full-blown drinking problem. The children would disappear at age six and only sometimes reappear in the summers for two months. Each time they came home there would be a new baby, nine kids in twelve years, some of them noticeably fetal alcohol, some not so much. The middle one was named Sarah, a pretty girl with long, thick, silky, dark hair and big brown eyes, easily angered and easily pacified. It was hard for Sarah to learn anything; what she learned one day could be gone from her head the next.

She was a victim of fetal alcohol syndrome, caused by Martha's drinking when she was pregnant. There were generations of people who drank and didn't know the connection between liquor and fetal development. Liquor at a certain stage of fetal development does irreversible damage; it leaves little holes in the brain where the synapses don't snap. Though Sarah didn't have the classic features of fetal alcohol, she was a victim of it nonetheless.

Sarah hated it at school, and she couldn't seem to do anything right. She was still learning the alphabet when some of her classmates were already reading. She was never able to read fluently and hated to be asked to read aloud. The only part of school she liked was cooking. At home she had been lovingly indulged, but at school she was harshly reprimanded and eventually beaten. None of that seemed to help: action and consequence couldn't be beaten into a mind unable to form the concept. In each of the first four years of Sarah's schooling, a sibling who came to the school in the fall never went home the next summer. Each year, Sarah stood with her oldest sister and the matron while they buried another brother. They all died of tuberculosis, which was rampant in the schools. In 1939, St Michael's in Alert Bay, Sarah's school, opened a "Preventorium" for the disease. The word must have been coined from "sanitorium," which is where adult TB patients went for treatment. The centre couldn't prevent the contagious disease, but it isolated those who contracted it and prolonged their lives with proper treatment.

Sarah's years of schooling were a long blur of sadness and beatings and humiliations. She wet the bed. She had never wet the bed before, but at the school she couldn't seem to wake up. Sometimes she'd even dream she was on the toilet, but morning after morning her sheets would be wet. She wanted to hide the evidence and at first was so embarrassed she made her bed up as if it was dry. If she was careful where she lay she could avoid the wet spot the next night. Soon the mattress was saturated and since she had the top bunk, the person below wasn't too happy. She had to take the lower bunk then, moving down with her own smelly mattress. After that the dorm supervisor made Sarah the object of daily inspection, and there were few mornings that she wasn't in trouble. She was made to wash her own sheets while everyone else had breakfast, and scrub the floor of the whole dorm while everyone else had outside play time.

When none of those things worked, the dorm supervisor and the matron began to wake her and plunge her—nightgown and all—into a tub of cold water as soon as the offence was noted. It was daily torture for Sarah, and she kicked and screamed and fought them. When this didn't work, they wrapped her urine-soaked sheet around her and made her wear it all day. No matter what the punishment, she wet the bed almost every night for two years. Her incontinence stopped as suddenly as it began, during the summer at home, but the damage to her self-esteem was permanent. She never again saw herself as worthy of anything, and she did enough to get by, no more. When she was twelve her dad died. He got TB too; Sarah knew he was going to die, and so did her mom. They both knew what the signs meant: the sunken pallor of his cheeks, the blood that he constantly coughed up, and the weakness that overcame him. Martha quit drinking to nurse him. When he died she asked God for forgiveness for her life and was reborn a Christian. She never drank again.

Not so with Sarah; she was a wild one. Martha had no idea how to deal with a rebellious thirteen-year-old. She pretty well left her to govern herself, and Sarah had no self-governance. By the time she was fourteen, she had taken the boat out of Kincolith and moved to Prince Rupert, moving in with a man much older than herself, relishing her freedom. By her fifteenth birthday she was starting to drink pretty heavily herself.

Jo is a firm believer in traditional foods and always has salmon and berries put away for the winter. One of the most treasured local wild berries is called huckleberry, and it's a rich feeling when there is a good supply of huckleberries in the freezer, a different kind of rich from having money. In the Hazeltons, the huckleberries are purported to grow three to five feet high, the bushes interspersed with blueberries growing to the same height, distinguished from each other by berry colour and shape. In the central interior, they both grow six to eighteen inches high, and you must crawl on the ground to pick them. They aren't abundant every year; sometimes a late frost will kill all the blossoms, sometimes hail will smash them to the ground just as they ripen, and sometimes the growing canopy of the forest makes it too shady for the berries to develop. They do best in logging clear-cuts, starting about the second year after logging and continuing till the new growth shades them too much. In the old days the people deliberately burned to create new berry patches. When it's a good year, we go out in groups.

In late summer there is a message on our phone. It's Jo, and it must be important for her to waste her precious minutes on an answering machine. Her voice, too loud for the phone, yells "Bingo berries! Phone me!" and she hangs up. I know what that means— there is a bumper crop in the Hazeltons. She's always bragged about the tall bushes that you can pick while standing, and now's the time to see how much she was exaggerating. I call my friend, Pam, and my daughter, Rena, who both pick too and arrange to drive up and back the next day. I call Jo back, and she tells me her friend said the berries were awesome. She gets excited when she finds out we're coming right away. She will be ready and waiting.

We leave early in the morning, Pam has a van and she says we'll take it, because the VW bug will be unable to carry all the berries we are going to pick. It takes us three and a half hours to get to the Hazeltons and another hour to find Jo's place. We drive to the wrong Hazelton—Old instead of South. We drive around and there is no address like she gave, nor anything close to it. We go to the town office and the clerk is puzzled: there is no street like that. Then a light comes on her face, and she says, "You want South! Go back to the highway and turn right, when you come to a fork in the road, there's a turning lane. Take it and you will drive through South town, and that's where you want to be."

I thank her and we follow her directions. When we get on the right street, I look for a blue tarp roof with tires on it. She said it's got twenty-eight tires on it now because every time it flapped, she climbed up and set another one on top. It's not hard to spot. Jo's waiting in the yard, buckets piled up, lunch packed—she's ready. She gives us a fast tour of her garden and yard. They're not really separate; there are mounds of soil with healthy-looking garden plants sharing space with three-foot-high grasses. It's very pretty in a sort of untamed way. Wild plants and cultivated ones are completely mixed together, and there isn't a row of anything anywhere. Everything is in mounds and clumps: there are several sculptures made from driftwood, climbing plants meandering up them. Footpaths run throughout, and there is a smooth spot with an iron heater. The short chimney attached and woodpile nearby attest to its use.

She shows us the raspberries on the north wall. They are spectacular, about eight feet tall and very healthy. She says she picked four gallons of berries off them. There are only eight plants, so that's quite impressive. We have a quick tour inside on our way to the bathroom. As soon as I walk in the door I recognize that musty odour; the smell on the clothing isn't from the second-hand store, it's from the trailer. It's probably moulding a bit because of the leaky roof. Jo's house reflects her artistic nature; everywhere there are beautiful things. I try to look past the bling factor and see the underlying structure. What I see is not so good. The front room side window has two interior 2x6 jack legs holding up a header that's supporting the roof. It's in line with the part that has no insulation, so the arch of the roof must have directed the water to the wall plate first and started rotting it. The interior support has been made into a shelf by Jo, pretty things hanging off it.

There is a wood cookstove in the kitchen, a wood heater in the addition. In the bathroom the toilet works, but you have to flush it with a bucket of water brought in from the kitchen sink. The bathtub and sink don't have water. Jo explains that there is a water leak, so she shut them off till she can find the time to get it fixed. I hear 'till she can afford it' because she's got lots of time.

We have to go back east on the highway to get on the logging road. Pam lets me drive her van; she says she doesn't like to drive on the logging roads. Her van is fun to drive, kind of zippy, and we make good time. The thing about logging roads is that they change with each season's cutting blocks, and what seemed to be a main road last time may not necessarily be one now. We stop at a couple major intersections and Jo takes a stab at what she feels is the proper way. A couple kilometres past one of these big crossings we stop the van and get out to scout around. Immediately we find berries, on chest-high bushes, exactly as promised by Jo. We stuff the first handfuls in our mouths: they are so good. It's hard to describe the taste, midway between tart and sweet, maybe a wonderful combination of the two.

Jo says, "It's a taste of heaven."

Someone or something has been ahead of us through this patch. There are a few bushes that they missed that are heavy with fruit, but most bushes seem creamed. There is bear scat in piles on the road as big as horses make. "Grizzly bear," Jo says. "He got here before us." We go back to the van, and Jo tells me to turn around and take the other fork that we just passed. We drive down that way and suddenly Jo knows exactly where we are. "We found it!" she announces. "This is where I wanted us to come."

We drive past another van, empty of people, and park about a half mile past them. We are in a large clear-cut. About a mile away the coastal trees made a dark green line clearly delineating the forest edge. "We pick near the centre. Keep close to each other and make noise so the grizzlies hear us," Jo instructs.

It isn't hard for us to make lots of noise. We are all kindred spirits, and the patch is so loaded with berries we can pick close enough to talk. Pam grew up in New Zealand. She's never quite lost that accent, and she has a droll way of looking at things that always makes us laugh. Jo has provided us with hand rakes; they are made with metal fingers poking forward from a box, with a bag attached to the open bottom for the berries to roll in. You scrape the branches from underneath with a combing motion. The leaves are supposed to fall through the screen on the side of the box as they roll in, but in actuality most of the leaves are gathered with the berries. We find we can pick an incredible amount in a short time, and in four hours we have every container we brought filled with berries. We figure it out: we've picked thirty-two gallons of berries in four hours. Two gallons an hour for each of us—that is incredible. We have purple hands, purple teeth, purple lips. We are a proud bunch when we stop in New Town for gas. All of us go in to the store, and we buy ice cream to top off the berries, laughing like fools and flashing our purple smiles at everyone.

Usually we are all fastidious pickers, making sure leaves and twigs don't end up in the buckets with the berries. We drive home the same night and set to cleaning the berries the next morning. Jo told us to take them outside in the wind and pour them on a blanket, then two people grab the blanket and gently toss the berries in the air and the wind blows the leaves away. Sounds so easy. We follow her instructions, but our berries are a little bit crushed from bouncing down the logging road when the tubs were so full, and maybe a little sideways crush when the van started skittering around on one sharp corner, then they sat overnight, and now they're sticking together in a glob and won't perform the toss in the air procedure at all. We start cleaning them the way we usually do, dumping them on a towel atop the table and rolling the berries off, but they are sticky and the leaves roll too. It takes almost an hour per gallon and is tedious work. We decide to save the leaves, it turns out they are a valuable ingredient for tea. By noon we're only half done, and it's taken us longer to clean them than to pick them. That kind of sucks. We ponder a better method, deciding to wash them first so they're not so sticky. We pour water directly into the Rubbermaid tub and to our surprise the leaves all float. We skim off the leaves and put them out to dry on a rack. In no time at all we're finished—I phone Jo and tell her how easy it is, and she says she knew that, didn't she tell us?

Carrying the hurt

* Simply worn out

Sarah met the man she would marry when she was sixteen. It was at a house party, and he said he'd drive her home. He didn't: he parked on the hill overlooking the bay and they made love in the car. She didn't go back to the house where she'd been living except to pack her clothes. She moved in with Wayne right away. They'd gone to the same school and remembered each other. "I always wanted to know you," he told her. "You were the prettiest one in the school."

Sarah remembered him only vaguely. She'd finished in grade seven and had only barely noticed the boys as separate entities, tucked into their corner of the school. She lied to him. "I thought you were the best-looking one of the guys, too."

With this mutual admiration they set up house, and within the first four years they had three children. Sarah was very good with the children as babies who could be soothed, but if they cried or became rebellious she no longer knew what to do with them. She was worn out, exhausted, and the only thing that seemed to give her relief was alcohol. She started drinking every day; it was easier to tolerate the noise and confusion that way. It wasn't long before she needed the liquor as much as she needed food. Without it she got sick, real sick. She called it her "medicine."

It was hard to find the extra money for the liquor, but if she went to the bar she often found someone willing to pay for a few drinks. She started spending a lot of time in the bar. She'd leave four-year-old

Trina to watch her two brothers, James, who at two was willing to play for hours by himself, and Don, who was still in the crib. She met a white guy in the bar. He was German, with light hair and blue eyes, handsome and generous, and seemed to really like her, unlike her husband who'd moved out shortly after the last baby was born. The day she came home from the bar and all the children were gone, she was arrested and charged with child abandonment. She spent a short time in jail, and when she was released she went to the bar, met her boyfriend, and went home with him. He lived in Smithers.

She got pregnant again right away, and Sam was born. She never quit drinking entirely, but she slowed down enough to only damage her unborn fetus a slight bit; same with the next. She called her little girl Jo. Her new husband wanted so much from her, much more than she could give. He wanted her to stay in the house all the time and watch the babies; he wanted her to cook and clean; and he wasn't near as much fun as when he'd been visiting in Rupert. She only went to church with him once, and not one of the women even said "hello" or looked her in the eye. It was obvious to her that she wasn't welcome there. She started going to the bar in Telkwa every once in a while. One day, her old man came home and found the kids alone, and he waited for her with an ultimatum: she had to either be a mother or not. She chose not and caught the first ride back to Rupert she could. At least in Rupert she knew everyone and could live the way she wanted. She became a fixture in the local bar, and there she drank the rest of her life away.

United Church apology

The government has weighed in: On behalf of the citizens of Canada, we are sorry that we didn't treat the Natives fairly. The churches have been weighing in, too. The United Church was the first to start apologizing: they sure should because they ran the Alberni School. It's bad enough that such cruelties existed, but the fact that those cruel, criminal, sadistic people were the personifications of church and God makes it even worse. There were two formal apologies issued by the United Church, the first one by Rt. Rev. Robert Smith in 1986, twenty-two years before the government issued theirs. Smith said:

Long before my people journeyed to this land your people were here, and you received from your Elders an understanding of creation and of the Mystery that surrounds us all that was deep, and rich, and to be treasured.

We did not hear you when you shared your vision. In our zeal to tell you of the good news of Jesus Christ we were closed to the value of your spirituality.

We confused Western ways and culture with the depth and breadth and length and height of the gospel of Christ.

We imposed our civilization as a condition for accepting the gospel.

We tried to make you be like us and in doing so we helped destroy the vision that made you what you were. As a result you, and we, are poorer and the image of the creator in us is twisted, blurred, and we are not what we are meant by God to be.

We ask you to forgive us and to walk together with us in the Spirit of Christ so that our peoples may be blessed and God's creation healed.

This apology was acknowledged but not accepted by the All Native Circle Conference in 1988. How could the Church still think Jesus Christ was good news for the Natives? How could the Church measure in four dimensions, even if "depth" or "breadth" means "width"? Are they trying to make two or, at best, three-dimensional thinking seem like four? A condition of acceptance—how about an unconditional imposition! Still wanting everyone to walk in the Spirit of Christ!! Christ sure as hell didn't help those little children. A line from a church song runs through my head—Jesus loves the little children—was he napping while generations of Native children were being abused?

They made a second apology, offered twelve years after the first, after the United Church heard testimony of terrible abuse from so many victims of the residential school system. The Church could no longer avoid facing blame for the offences committed.

The second apology sounds more sincere. It was offered by the Right Reverend Bill Phipps, moderator of the United Church of Canada. In it he said, "We know that many within our church will still not understand why each of us must bear the scar, the blame for this horrendous period in Canadian history. But the truth is, we are the bearers of many blessings from our ancestors, and therefore, we must also bear their burdens."

He said the Church commits itself to "never again use the power of the Church to hurt others with attitudes of racial and spiritual superiority."

That is a laudable commitment, although too bad he didn't say the Church would teach its members not to have those very attitudes.

The Church apologizes because its members feel they have sinned by commission and omission—doing something bad and not speaking out against it when they knew it was bad.

"Body and Health" at Canada.com says "epilepsy" is a Greek word meaning "to be seized," which is exactly how Jo described it. The seizures are caused by a sudden and abnormally high discharge of electrical activity in the brain. Epilepsy is not a disease; it is a symptom of a brain dysfunction. Think of an arc from an electrical short or a miniature lightning storm inside your head; 1 per cent of the population gets it when they're young, and another 2 per cent get it after they're completely grown. It is a trait that can be passed on genetically or it can be acquired because of an abnormality in development. There are lots of things that trigger seizures and lots of medications to suppress them, some effective, some not—it's kind of a personal thing—most of them have some nasty side effects, the most common being mental sluggishness, increased facial hair growth, and higher rates of birth defects. I wonder if that's where Jo's heavy mustache came from; the medicines must be some kind of hormone therapies. Nowhere do they say smoking pot might be a way to control seizures. I wonder if Jo might be a medical pioneer? I Google "pot smoking controls epilepsy" and I get 955,000 different sites. Maybe the pioneering thing was a tad premature.

Jo says she doesn't know when she got epilepsy. She can't remember having it when she was little, but by the time she was a teenager she was having seizures all the time. It made it hard to have friends; it's embarrassing to wake up from a seizure, sometimes with soiled underwear, not knowing what happened. It takes a loyal friend to stick with you, loving family members to deal with it; Jo found there weren't many of either. She remembers her first summer job at the Tastee-Freez. It was so much fun; she waited tables and brought the meals, but the cash was collected by the owner's wife who sat behind the till every hour the restaurant was open. She remembers the camaraderie of the staff and how much fun it was for the few short weeks she worked there. I ask what happened. Tears form in her eyes, hurt reflected forward thirty-five years. "Two grand mal seizures, two days in a row. They were really nice about it, but they said they had to let me go."

I feel such pity for her, but she doesn't like pity parties any more than I do, and she senses my feeling right away. "Fuck off," she says, then grins. "Do you know who Wab Kinew is?"

"No."

"He's a CBC guy. He's more than that, he's a wise old man in a young, good-looking body. He's really smart and in tune with what's going on, and he says the Native people alive today are not victims, we are the survivors. That's what I am, Janet, I am a survivor. I am who I am because my life made me this way, and I don't need to stand in anyone's shadow. I'm as good a person as the next. I'm not a victim of epilepsy, nor of abuse—I'm a survivor of them. I got two good legs and I stand on 'em."

"You go, girl," I tell her. "You're Miss Nisga'a Survivor!"

Jo shakes her head. "I don't know nothing about being Nisga'a. I know more about Wet'suwet'en. Those people in Moricetown, they were the ones who looked at us and really saw us. I tell you, when I was young there were boxes of fish left on our doorstep and bags of hand-me-downs. The dresses fit me and the stuff for Sam fit him. Those people never hung around for us to thank them. They weren't doing it for the thanks, they were doing it because they were looking out for us. I know Wet'suwet'en people, and that's what I know. That's what I like—how they made sure we had the basics. They looked out for us and we weren't even from there."

"There are no good foster homes. At least none of the ones I went to."

"Oh, come on. There must be good ones. Look at Bev." My niece is a foster mother, and I think the kids she looks after are pretty lucky to find a home with as much love as hers.

"That's the exception, not the rule. The ones I went to did it for the money, I swear that's the only reason. I can't say I ever felt like any foster home wanted me. I was simply a way for them to get money. I never felt love from anywhere I was sent. I won't say they mistreated me everywhere; that's not true. Some places were worse than others; that is for sure true. I moved around a bit. I was never happy in any of those places, that's mostly what I remember. I missed my dad and Sam, and I even missed my uncle. They were my world, they were the ones that loved me, and I can tell you a person can live without lots of things but when love is missing, that's when a person suffers. When I look back on all those years, they blur together. I couldn't tell you now who some of those people even were. All I wanted that whole time was to go back to my own family. I was never happy till I went back home."

"You never got to visit? All those years? You never saw your dad or your brother?"

"No. A couple times I tried to run away and find them. I wasn't very old, and they caught me pretty quick. They told me that if I found my dad and he got caught with me, they'd send him to jail. When we went to court I found out it wasn't true, and that lady had no business saying that. I think—I hope—she lost her job over it. All I wanted, that whole time, was my family back."

Jo says, "You know, there are moments in your life that change how things go for you forever. Wouldn't it be nice if you recognized those moments when they're happening? So you could pay more attention?"

When Jo got her family back, she was thirteen and pretty well finished with school. Her dad said she didn't have to go to school anymore, but she had to make herself useful and that she did, taking on the cooking and cleaning, not just at home but for hire as well, doing odd jobs and simply being content to be home with her dad and Sam again. She hated school anyway and was never going to be able to pass math. Math was her downfall, her brain foe; she couldn't seem to get it, hadn't passed a math quiz for years. She finally had money figured out, and numbers up to a hundred. She knew that past hundreds there were thousands then millions, but those numbers seemed like a well too deep to draw from. Presenting Jo with a rudimentary algebra problem was like giving it to the wind, blowing the concept away while she tried to figure out how they expected her to add the friggin' alphabet. She could read well and she contented herself with that; she read everything that presented itself. Picking up a book and sliding into another person's world for a while had been a welcome escape through the years that she'd been fostered out. She often thought about how wonderful it was, that everything a person wanted to know was written down somewhere—the collective knowledge of mankind all written—it was simply a matter of finding the right book.

Her uncle had moved away, so it was Sam and Dad who she lived with. They'd been up at Rupert working at the fish plant during the summer and now they were all back in the Hazeltons. There was a guy who she was seriously attracted to. He was twenty-four, and he'd been coming out to visit her dad for a few weeks. He wanted to know if she wanted to go to a movie? Did she? Yes! She sure did.

That was the beginning of her first relationship. At first, he treated her like a little sister, but the feelings she had for him were anything but sisterly. It was only a matter of months before they were having sex, and only a few more before she was pregnant. Jo was horrified when she found out she was pregnant. She really didn't know how people got pregnant, but she was pretty sure they had to be married. Her dad had made her go to the doctor because she was so sick every morning. When the doctor told him she was pregnant he didn't speak to her; the drive home was one long streak of silence. At home he cracked a twenty-sixer and drank till it was gone.

Her dad must've told her boyfriend because she didn't have to say anything: he knew. He said they'd get married but didn't say when. Jo hoped it would be soon, but she didn't ask. That fall her dad drank heavily; he was a pretty cheerful drunk, and he had lots of friends. Her boyfriend came out every day; he liked drinking with her dad, and this one day, another old friend they hadn't seen for a while stopped by early in the morning. The men had whiskey in their coffee for breakfast. They cooked eggs and gave a good feed to the friend's dog, named Sheba, a big friendly German shepherd. After breakfast, they decided to go down to the river and get some trout. Jo had been hungry for trout for weeks. They parked on the road and walked in to a spot where the river channel came close to the shore on a curve with lots of rapids. There was a rock face to the left with a pool below where trout gathered. On the right, the face went straight down to the rapids below, and it was easy to cast into the fast water from the high bank and reel in through the pool.

It was like a party, the men drinking and reminiscing while they fished. Jo and her boyfriend explored short distances up and down the river, but the only good spot for fishing was right where they were. They went back on top with the men and—to this day Jo doesn't know how—she lost her footing. Suddenly, she was reeling on the edge of the rock and just as suddenly falling. It seemed an eternity between the beginning of the fall and hitting the water; clearly she heard her dad's panicked voice yelling, "Jo!" She heard a high-pitched giggle from her boyfriend, and the command of her dad's friend, "Go get her, Sheba." Then she was fighting for her life in the cold water of the Bulkley. She had fallen directly into the rapids, and she was tumbled ass over teakettle again and again. Sometimes she could power her head above the water and take in a gasping breath of air, but then she would take another hit and be tumbled about. She didn't see the dog coming but felt when she arrived, felt the teeth grasp onto her fingers, then onto her forearm, then her shoulder as the dog helped get her to where the current finally let go. She crawled out of the water and collapsed, hacking out water and gasping for air. The dog stayed right with her, licking her and whining till the men arrived.

The men were shocked into sobriety by the seriousness of the moment. They wrapped her in a blanket, and she couldn't stop trembling. They took her home and lit the fire, but she still couldn't stop; she shook so violently her teeth were rattling together. Black and blue bruises were starting to show up all over. There didn't seem to be a square inch of skin surface that didn't have a bruise. Even her face was swelling up. In her ears was the echo of that giggle. What the hell did that mean, that giggle? She couldn't stop hearing it. Her dad got in the car to go get help, and he arrived back within the hour with his friend who was a lifeguard. It seemed an unusual choice but turned out to be correct. He was familiar with both the injuries and the trauma of river accidents. He called her a good fighter, told her most people would be dead if they tried to go through those rapids with no lifejacket, said she was a trooper, felt down all her limbs, and said nothing was broken and she would recover.

Before the bruises were even faded he made Jo come with him to the river where it was calm, stepped with her out into the current, and they swam together. He told her, "It's just like falling off a horse; a person has to get right back on or they will always be scared. A person usually remembers what happened last time." Jo wasn't scared of the water that day; her fears were deeper than that. She was scared of the laugh. That laugh that echoed through her head until it killed love. From that day on, she couldn't summon any good feeling for her boyfriend: there was one big lump of hurt in the place where the love had been. When she told him she didn't want to see him anymore he nodded and was gone. It was obvious to her he didn't love her either.

Jo carried that hurt around a long time. Now, in mid-life, she looks back on it and forgives. "I didn't know that some people laugh when they're distraught until I was older. Now when I look back I see he could have had some entirely different motive than what I attributed to him, and I'm not mad at him anymore."

The boyfriend leaving cleared the way for another man who had had his eye on Jo. He was younger than the last one, almost twenty-one, and he asked her on a date. He'd just moved back from Edmonton where he'd been going to school to learn accounting and already had a job in an office in Smithers. He was smart and good-looking and they got along so well but the only thing was, Jo couldn't figure out how to tell him she was going to have a baby. She was almost five months along and hardly showed. Finally she gathered her courage up in a ball and told him the sad truth. He didn't react in any of the ways she had imagined, rejection being the core that all her imaginations had revolved on. He was silent for a long time, then he asked her if she wanted to get married. Hell, yeah! She sure did.

The doctrine of discovery

The Catholic Church has sort of apologized for their part in the residential school fiasco. Pope Benedict XVI made a carefully worded apology for the abuse suffered in the schools and was heard by Phil Fontaine.

He didn't apologize for the schools themselves, but for the abuse suffered in said schools. Here's what the Canadian Conference of Catholic Bishops had to say about it:

"Approximately 16 out of 70 Catholic dioceses in Canada were associated with the former Indian Residential Schools, in addition to about three dozen religious communities. Each diocese and religious community is legally responsible for its own actions. The Catholic Church as a whole was not associated with the Residential Schools, nor was the Canadian Conference of Catholic Bishops."

It makes it sound like the heads didn't know what their hands were doing.

That research rolls around to the Doctrine of Discovery, and that's when the bigger picture emerges. All the history in high school was learning about how we discovered this land and became nations, Canada and United States. We learned which Europeans discovered which places and memorized the dates when it happened. Apparently, before Europeans came here there was no history, or none that was taught in any of my high school years. No one explained the Doctrine of Discovery, and what they really meant by "discovery." The meaning of this is far different from what you might suppose: the doctrine of discovery is what *allowed*—no, that's not quite the right word—it's what *promoted* and *encouraged* Christian countries to send ships to anywhere in the world that Christians didn't live, and then land, plant their flags, and claim the people, their belongings, and their land for whatever Christian country the sailors happened to belong to. The Doctrine of Discovery went on to specifically tell the discoverer to "invade, search out, capture, vanquish, and subdue all Saracens and pagans whatsoever, and other enemies of Christ," and then on to tell the discoverer it was okay to take all their stuff and keep it and to render their persons to perpetual slavery. It was signed and sealed by the pope.

The text of the *Romanus Pontifex* or Papal Bull is on Wikipedia. It was written in 1455 by Pope Nicholas V, the supreme head of the Catholic Church and the "civilized" world. Holy crap! Papal Bulls are laws. In 1455, the Pope was the legal and secular leader, the absolute head of all civilized European Christian nations. They had been plundering along the coasts of Arabia and Africa for a while and were justifying it in the name of the Lord, hence their impatience with the "Saracens." They were evangelizing with weapons and living high on the proceeds. World commerce was all about who was shipping what from where, and all Christian countries had ships. They were in a race to plunder the world and they felt that it was their duty, by God, to do so. All the lands that they discovered would belong to the discoverer, and the takes were incredible. The Natives of every country lost almost every encounter. Mostly being peaceful tribes, they often were taken as slaves, with no human rights acknowledged, and their homelands invaded and stolen. This was all done by Christian countries because the pope said they could.

This is still law.

I keep reading and reading, trying not to believe that this is law. But it is. It was enshrined in US law in 1823, in a case called *Johnson v. McIntosh*. The court ruled that as a result of the law of 1455, the European "conquerers" could dispose of the land to the newly formed Americas with no input from the Native occupants who had no rights as non-Christians to title of their lands. They had only the right of occupancy, and that was at the whim of the Christian authorities who could expel them at any time.

In Canada, Australia, and New Zealand the legal authorities have in turn cited this case and made it law. That's why land claims are so hard to settle. The law of the land doesn't recognize the title of inherent right; the law recognizes the rights of discovery, conquest, and vanquishing, granted by a pope almost six hundred years ago. How sad is that?

There is another Papal Bull called the *Dum Diversas* written in 1452. It was written by the same pope and in some sites the two Bulls are used interchangeably. They say and mean the same thing to me.

Growing season

Now that Jo's a professional house-sitter, we have to book her in advance. We live out in the country on a farm with chickens, pigs, dogs, cats, horses, and plants that need everyday attention. Jo has been here enough to be familiar with all the stuff that needs to be done. She comes a few days early to do the rounds with us and learn what to do with the room full of plants. Her hands are still not good. She hasn't gone back to get the left hand fixed because the right one still isn't working that well. She can't even grip a coffee cup in it.

It's April and that's when we need to start all the plants for the garden and greenhouse. I have a room full of plants in plug-trays, a whole garden in miniature. Cabbage plants that will eventually grow to a three-foot circumference are started in two cubic inches of soil, seventy-two of them in a ten by twenty-two inch space. My age means I still think in feet and inches, although I do measure some things in metric. The room has a plywood and lumber shelf with four fluorescent lights and a twig shelf with four more. I made the shelves myself, not very pretty, but solid and functional. The twig one is against the window for extra light, and the centre of the room has a four-sided valley, its sides made of tiers of plants with a 1,000-watt grow light in the centre. You need sunglasses on if you're staying in that room for long. The lights are all on a timer, so Jo doesn't have to worry about that unless the power goes out. Then she'll have to reprogram the on and off times for the timer. Programming electrical stuff is not Jo's strong suit, so I write the steps out plainly and leave the paper by the timer.

What is crucial in this room is that the plants don't dry out. There is a lot of heat generated by the lights, and the plants can dry out fast, yet it's equally crucial that they don't get waterlogged. It's easy to overwater them because there are solid trays under the plugs so no water drips in the house. It's something a person learns over time, but I trust Jo. She has an eye for how the plant is feeling, and happy plants look good. It doesn't take much stress to make them unhappy, and I hope they all make it through my absence. It's hard to explain how I feel about these little plants. After laboriously planting the seeds with the point of a wet toothpick, one by one into each little compartment, I've watched impatiently as they've emerged through the soil. They contain the promise of future bounty, and they will eventually give up their life force to feed us. They're like my little friends. I'm worried maybe I spend too much time alone—my friends are plants and animals. I consign them all to Jo's care and leave knowing everything is in good hands, well—kind of screwed-up hands—but knowing everything is being carefully tended.

Jo sinks roots

The soil in Jo's garden is sandy, and left to itself it doesn't grow things all that well. She surveys the backyard in the spring and decides that she'd better make it more productive. She orders a couple truckloads of soil and ten round bales. The round bales are from her friend, an elderly farm woman, eighty years young, from whom she also buys her birch slab firewood; she offers some old hay she says isn't fit for animal consumption. She and Jo roll the bales off the flatbed truck and line them up in the front yard. The bales were poor when they were baled. The hay was rained on so much while it was supposed to be drying in the field that the grass turned black. Then it was optimistically rolled over on a hot day, only to blacken on the other side in turn after the next storm. The octogenarian says they baled it anyway to get the swaths off the field, and hoped for better the next year. Sitting out in the barnyard for two more years hasn't improved the appearance of the bales. They're so big they take up the whole front yard, five on each side of the drive. Another truck delivers the compost. Jo guides him between the trailer addition that she calls the "joy-shack" and the shed opposite, and the truck barely fits through. He dumps the load in the back corner of the yard, in easy reach of the places that most need it. Her neighbours aren't overly impressed. They think she's bringing down property values. Jo feels them looking down their noses at her and gossiping about her to each other. She has a laugh about that one on the phone. "Like they have valuable property! You could buy any place on this street for peanuts already." So with the neighbours peeking out their windows and over their fences with disapproval, Jo sets about doing some serious gardening. All her life she's wanted a place of her own and it's so nice to be able to do exactly as she wants in the yard. Her hands still aren't very strong, but she learns how to compensate, shovelling three two-foot-deep trenches across the backyard, piling the soil on top of the centre ridges and along the sides. Then she adds a foot of compost and plants on the resulting raised beds. The bales she tries to wrestle around, but can't make much headway. They are very hard to move.

Across the street a new guy has moved in, a truck driver. Jo's seen him out the window a few times, and to her it seems he looks nice, so one day when she's getting frustrated trying to move one of the bales and he's outside in his own yard, she does what for her is a very brave thing. She walks across the street, introduces herself, and asks him if he would mind giving her a hand for a moment. His name's Rusty and he quickly agrees to help her roll the bale into position, then helps roll two more tight together. Jo asks him if he'd like a drink of tea and they sit at the table in the yard for a while and visit. She decides he's as nice as he looks and is happy all afternoon after he leaves. She mounds compost in the crevice made by the bales touching side by side and plants squashes. She opens a few of the bales and mulches around the perennials and along the paths. It's a long and difficult task to spread the compost and hay around the yard but the results make it worth the effort. There will be more food than one person could possibly eat and a screen of greenery that makes the backyard a private place in summer.

Over the summer, Jo and Rusty become friends. That's all Jo wants from him, friendship. She's had enough of that intimate relationship that living together and marriage require. She doesn't even notice that her feet do an involuntary happy dance when she thinks about him. She says, "Rusty's nice, but he smokes like a chimney," and "the only place it's comfortable to visit with him is outside." She only invited him into the house once that first summer and when he asked if he could smoke in her house she was too polite to say no, but it stunk up her place so much she could still smell it days later. Her nose is still supersensitive; it had taken half the spring and some good hot fires in both stoves at once to get the stale smell from the wet roof out.

As the summer progresses and the garden grows lush, the neighbour's noses come down a hair. They can't help but notice how good everything looks. Jo looks back over the fences and can't help but notice that she's got better results. The compost is so rich that the plants jump out of the ground, and the hay mulch that she spread so generously keeps her sandy soil moist during the dog days of summer. Jo finds that she can eat well from the bounty in her backyard, and her grocery bill shrinks to a new low. She makes sure every visitor leaves with produce and she shares with the neighbours.

She's made some good friends. One is a Filipina woman named Mimi, who bakes and cans for the farmers' market. Jo is always willing to share her garden bounty with Mimi. Jo loves Hazelton, loves the winter with its snow and freezing, loves the melt in the spring. She treats herself to getting up early, being outside when the sun peeks over the edge of the mountain to bathe the slopes with its golden glow, watches the light race down the hills to the town lying quietly below. Hardly anyone else on the street gets up early, so Jo likes to think the mornings belong to her.

Finally she can make the last payment on the place. It'll leave her flat-ass broke, but it'll be worth it. She's wanted to stop roaming around, wants to have a place where it's okay to grow old, a place where her roots can sink, where the effort she puts into improvements won't be left behind in the next move. There won't be a next move; she's staying put. Jo knows that she has to have a lawyer handle the property transfer, and preferably one who will do it for practically nothing because that's what she'll have left after paying out the house. She doesn't know if there are property taxes owing; she doesn't know how any of that stuff works, or if there are any liens on it. She phones around and finds out about a legal aid lawyer who practises in town twice a week. She makes an appointment to see him and he agrees to do the job for seventy-five dollars. That she can afford, not the six hundred quoted by the other lawyer she'd phoned. It takes three weeks, but finally the wonderful day arrives when she holds the deed in her hand. She only holds it for a minute, then hands it back to the lawyer. "I don't want to keep it. Can you put it in a safe place?"

The Hazeltons' greatest appeal is to the senses: the setting is pure beauty. The towns are in the Hazelton mountain range, close enough to the coast to give the area a warm climate, almost always warmer than the same latitude further inland. The scenery is spectacular; from Jo's front room window Mount Roche De Boule dominates the landscape. The Seven Sisters' peaks are further away, but the skyline is ridged with awesome mountains. Driving west on Highway 16 you can sense a change around Moricetown, the air suddenly seems coastal.

In South Town, nothing ever seems to change. Little things maybe: some people move away, some move back, a few new ones come, but it seems none of the basics change. No new houses get built, services seem to only go downhill. Most of the stores closed, and now a person has to drive to Smithers or Old Town to go shopping. The area is depressed. Jo doesn't have a car, but almost everyone else has one, so she doesn't have any trouble getting into town when she needs to. Sometimes she catches a ride with a friend or neighbour, sometimes on the bus, and sometimes with the unofficial taxi. You have to pay twenty bucks but he'll drive you around and wait outside and then drive home, so he's worth it.

The Hazeltons have a lot more issues: there is hardly any work locally and there are the same drug and alcohol problems that so many northern towns have, complete with the social issues they cause, including a very high teen suicide rate. Jo takes each one to heart. It makes her cry every time, and she wishes there was something she could do for them, some way to help them see how precious each and every person on the face of this earth is.

Throughout the fall, Jo gets depressed. The trailer that in summer had seemed her liberation from wandering now feels more like a trap. It was one thing in the summertime to compensate for her lack of finger dexterity when gardening was her main pursuit, but it's quite another altogether to compensate inside during the winter. Jo's hobbies, which have become part of her life-support, are beadwork and quilting. She can't do either one; her hands won't grip the needle for more than a couple minutes before they cramp up and refuse to co-operate. She gets so broke that she swallows her pride and goes to the social services office. It takes her ten minutes to get in to see the woman, and she can't even look her in the eye. Jo says she needs some money to live on, tells her she's so broke she can't afford food. The woman asks her where she lives, how much her rent is, and when and where did she last work? She wants to know if Jo might qualify for employment insurance, which is the new name for unemployment insurance. She is surprised to find out Jo hasn't worked for over a year and wonders out loud how she managed this long. Jo feels guilty, like she's done something wrong by surviving. When she finds out Jo was on short-term disability she gets on the phone and calls someone else. After she hangs up the phone she is silent for a while. Then she says, "Usually people who own their homes don't qualify."

"You mean you make people choose—you can have a home or you can have food, but you can't have both?" Jo feels tears of indignation pooling up, she isn't going to beg anymore—this was a bad idea. She stands up to leave.

"I'm simply telling you the rules, Ma'am. We have to follow procedures and rules. You may end up qualifying. I'll get you the forms." Jo can hear censure in her voice and feels dirty, like she picked up a layer of dirt when she walked in the door and she can't wait to get away. "I'll starve to death first," she vows internally as she politely accepts the forms. When she gets home she doesn't even read them. She crumples them up one by one and places them under the kindling. They aren't even burnt up when the phone rings and the preacher asks her if she can house-sit for him right away—he has a family emergency.

Jo phones mid-winter, and finally she admits that her hands aren't getting any better. She's learned a whole lot about prevention, taken shark cartilage and a half a dozen other herbal supplements which all improve the condition slightly but not enough to actually say they're getting better and not worse. She is pinning her hopes on this doctor, the same specialist who operated last time, who still believes he can do an operation that will significantly improve the functioning of her hands.

"This time I want you to do them both at once," she tells him.

"That's not a good idea. If we do one at a time you will still have the other to work with while it heals."

"I might not come back for the second, and I can't work worth a shit now. If I have time to think it over I might not come back—that's what happened last time."

The doctor looks at her, knows her enough now to know she's serious. "We maybe could do it in a series, day surgeries with a local anesthetic, fix those two little fingers first and then the rest at once. Do you have someone to look after you for the first few weeks?"

· "I sure do. I'm booked in at a resort," she says although in actuality she is staying with us at the farm. I offered as soon as I knew she was going to go get her hands fixed. The doctor is going to help her get on disability again. There are a whole bunch more forms she has to fill out, some the doctor fills out, and she needs a reference letter from someone else saying she needs it. Would I write it for her? Of course I will.

She arrives on the bus, laden down as always. She's been taking garlic to build up her immune system so she can breeze through these operations. It's coming out her pores and creating a cloud around her that no insect or virus could possibly penetrate; it takes a staunch friend to ignore it. I try to, but poor Rick can't. The next day it's no different. We go to Prince George for the day and he leans away when she pokes her head through the bucket seats to chat on the way to town and he doesn't walk with us in the stores. She tells me she's been eating a whole bulb of raw garlic every day and I miss the opportunity to suggest she maybe use something less stinky to boost her immune system.

Jo eats healthy. She eats very little bread, doesn't drink milk or soft drinks, and doesn't do sugar. She likes basic foods: vegetables, fruits, nuts, and meat. She's really healthy except for this hand thing. We sure hope the operations will do some permanent good, but she reminds me it didn't last time.

"But you didn't finish last time—this time you're going for the full meal deal. This time it's going to be good."

"He said I wouldn't be able to do anything for at least a week till the stitches come out. I'm not even supposed to try to bend them."

"You better ask him if you'll still be able to wipe your own ass. There are certain things I don't do," I say, because it's true.

"Don't worry—I won't be asking you to do that!" she laughs and we are clear on that subject.

Each time, I drive her to town for the day surgery, then home again all bandaged up. Now she gets the prescription for the pain medication filled before we leave town, but hardly needs it. She says she can feel the little fingers all the way up to where they join on her elbows. By the time one gets healed up and working, it's time to do the next. The grand finale is the day she gets the palms on both hands done. She looks grey and spaced out when she comes out. She tells me she watched them doing it, gives a disgusting blow-by-blow description that could make the squeamish upchuck. I don't want to hear it, and I hold up my hand to stop her but she ignores me.

"It's so cool, you can see it, scrape, scrape, scrape he goes."

"Are you on very good drugs?"

"No, just painkiller. My hands are still kind of froze. Scrape, scrape," she giggles. "Make 'em smooth, make 'em slide."

Her painkiller is well named; she's sure not feeling any pain, but later when the freezing wears off she's ready for more painkillers. It's crazy, getting both hands done at once, even after the cuts heal and the stitches come out. She's got a house-sitting job booked for one month after the last operations and when it comes time she can bend her hands, both of them, into fists, but same as last time she has no strength in either one. Twisting is the worst; trying to undo a jar lid or wring out a cloth is a painful process for both her and anyone watching. She thinks she will be fine because the job really is house-sitting, and there are no other chores to do.

Married

Getting married when you're fifteen isn't easy. A person that age is not old enough to sign the papers, still not old enough to make mature decisions. Jo's dad couldn't sign for her: he never married her mother and how could he prove he was even her father? She was underage and the only person who could sign the paper allowing the marriage was her mother. She knew her mother lived in Prince Rupert. Her dad gave Jo an address where she might find her or someone who knew her, so she got on the Greyhound and headed to Rupert.

Jo got off the bus downtown and asked for directions to the address from the lady at the bus station counter. She walked through town marvelling at the way the houses were perched on the hill, long stairways connecting the front doors to the streets. The place was at the edge of town and it seemed like she'd walked a long way when the number finally appeared. It stopped her feet; she stood on the street and stared at the house for some time before climbing the rickety stairs to knock on the faded blue door. She climbed slowly, wondering what she'd say. As she was raising her hand to knock the door opened, she froze with her hand in the knocking position, staring at the person who opened the door. Very short, a round face with puckered lips like her teeth were missing, blue polka-dot kerchief wrapped around her head, long dress with apron over the top: the impression was one of age, old age. Jo stared in disbelief. "Sarah?" she said it like a question.

The response was laughter. "Come in, come in. No child, I'm not Sarah. Come in," she repeated as Jo stood indecisively on the porch. Jo stepped inside and gratefully accepted the cup of coffee that was placed in front of her. "Now what do you want with Sarah?" Jo found herself explaining that she needed a paper signed, that Sarah was her mother. The crone nodded along. "You don't say?" she kept saying. "Where are you from?" she asked when Jo was silent. "Telkwa? You're one of those kids from Telkwa? You know she got put in jail for leaving those kids here from Rupert?"

Jo shook her head. No, she didn't know. The crone nodded, agreeing with herself. "Yep. That's what happened. But she isn't in jail now for that; she's in the drunk tank. They picked her up this afternoon from the pub; she was causing a big ruckus. She'll be easy to find in jail, but they probably won't let her out till Monday, though. You can stay here and wait."

"Thanks, no, I think I'll go see if they'll let me in. I don't want to wait till Monday."

Jo walked to the police station, her steps measuring equal parts of hope and dread. At the station she explained her mission. The man behind the counter seemed friendly and she kept talking till he held up his hand and asked, "Are you pregnant?"

Jo looked down, wondering how he knew. She nodded, just one short nod. He sighed, then said, "Your mother is in custody. She's sleeping it off and won't wake for a long time. I can see you need her but she isn't responsible. Let me see what I can do." He rose and left the room with her papers. Jo barely had time to look around the office before he was back, papers signed. "There you go," he said. "Have a nice life."

Jo stared at the paper in disbelief. There it was. "Sarah McNeil" signed across the bottom in clear, strong writing. It was witnessed by himself and he proceeded to stamp his credentials overtop his signature before handing it over. Jo left the station weighed down with equal parts of regret and relief. All the things that she'd planned to say to her mother when she finally saw her were still just plans, and it felt like such a letdown. The reality of her mother in the drunk tank was tough to take: in all the imaginations of her life her mother had played a nobler role. The relief of avoiding what could only have been painful and the fact of the signed document in her hand kept her going forward. She was halfway home before she started wondering how the paper got signed so quickly and only a few miles further along before she decided the cop must have signed it himself. He didn't have time to go wake up her mother and get her to sign a paper. He had to have done it himself. Jo didn't know how she felt about that, but it seemed like the first time in her life that the police had ever helped her and almost seemed like a good omen.

The rototiller

One of the tools I use gardening is a Rototiller. For years, I used an eight-horse, wheel-driven Troy-Bilt. It's a ground-chewing wonder, but it's heavy and awkward to turn. When a machine gets old and needs a minimum of a half-hour's persuasion by a mechanic each time to get it running, it's time to replace it. This time Honda is looking good: those little engines start and run like a dream. "Sell a Honda, lose a customer—they never come back," says the dealer. The one that looks good has a six-horse motor and the whole unit is smaller and lighter. They have one in the rental shop in Vanderhoof, and it makes sense to rent it and see how well it works. It costs twenty-five bucks for the day, and it sure does a nice job. I till up the whole garden in one day, just to get my money's worth.

I order a brand new one from the dealer . They say it'll take a couple months to get it in, but it doesn't matter, the only thing we could till right now are snowballs. As long as it's in by spring, it's good. It comes in early February, just after Jo comes for all the hand operations, and she comes with me to pick it up. We unload the tiller and park it in the carport where I pat it occasionally. It doesn't hurt to be kind to inanimate, helpful objects.

By the beginning of May it's dry enough to start tilling. The weather has been really nice and the garden soil is firming up. The Rototiller fires up first pull; that Honda engine is nice. The tiller has some safety features built in, a little different from the Troy-Bilt, but simple nonetheless. It won't go into reverse with the tines in gear. That's good, you can't run over yourself and if you let go of it in forward gear the tines stall, also good.

I put it in first gear and engage the tines, then push it down into the soil. It takes a hell of a jump forward. I let go, and it stops and sits there innocently idling. That's weird: I'm sure the machine I rented would have dug in here but the soil is a little harder now, packed down from the snow melt. Maybe a person needs to hang on to it a little better and push down harder. This time the machine jumps forward again, but I'm ready. I jump with it and jam it down hard. It responds by leaping up in the air and forward about six feet. I am pulled off my feet and don't let go of it till we land. It lands on its front, blades churning. I land on my feet, unfortunately right on top of the rotating blades, and then I let go. There is a sudden, huge pain in my left leg: the tiller walked up it before it died. I turn and hobble into the house, I need help. I phone my sister who lives less than a mile away. "I hurt myself. Come and get me," I say to her, then pass out on the floor.

Rene and her husband both come, which is a good thing because now I can't put any weight on the leg at all. They take me into the hospital emergency where the leg gets X-rayed. It's not broken, just chewed up. I get stitches and a tetanus shot and released. The doctor wonders out loud why someone would rototill with no safety boots on. I tell him my feet are fine, it's my leg that's screwed. He just lifts his eyebrows.

On the way home we wonder why the Rototiller acted like that, and my brother-in-law says maybe the tines are on backwards, he'll check when we get back. He does, and sure enough the tines are on backwards. We discuss it, saying things like, "Well, I wonder how many more tillers got sent out from the factory like that?"

I decide I'd better phone Honda and tell them someone at their factory is making a big mistake. I get customer service, tell them what happened, and tell them the serial number of my tiller and that they'd better do some checking. They tell me they will take care of it. I feel like I've saved other people from going through this same misery.

Rick dispels that illusion when he gets home. "I'd be mighty surprised if the tines were installed at the factory. Tillers come to the dealer in a box, not completely assembled. I'll bet you the dealer put them on like that."

"No!" I say. "I talked to customer service, he didn't tell me that."

Rick looks at me like I'm simple. "Do you really think they would?"

I phone another Honda dealer and ask him how rototillers come? Tines mounted or not?

Not is the answer.

This doesn't seem quite right: maybe they've mislabelled customer service, maybe it should be called "dealer protection."

I phone the dealer where I bought my tiller, and they already know what's happened, the guy from customer service has talked to them. "How do we know you didn't change them around yourself?" the dealer wonders. "How do we know you didn't try to till in third gear? Or try to till on the road surface? There are safety features built in. Why didn't you let go?"

This is pissing me off. "I didn't change them myself, I was in first gear, and I was in the garden. I didn't let go because I was trying to till. This happened because you put the tines on backwards," I say in an angry voice.

"Reversing the tines is a legitimate way to operate the tiller," they tell me.

"I've been gardening for better than twenty years, all of them with the help of a tiller and in no instance have I ever heard of anyone tilling with the tines on backwards."

"We will come and pick up the tiller, fix it for you," they offer.

I'm out of commission for a few weeks anyway so I agree, but I'm angry with them because it is their fault that I'm hurt and so far they don't seem to be taking any responsibility for it. An old guy comes to get the tiller, and I hobble out on my crutches to watch him load it. He came in a pickup and he sets out a ramp and fires up the tiller, puts it in gear and heads for the truck. What he doesn't notice is that the tines are still in gear. If they touch down even once on the ramp, we are going to have a repeat of the flying tiller incident with another operator. I start shrieking to be heard over the tiller, and when he looks over I make a cutting motion. To my relief he shuts it off. "The tines are in gear!" I shout. He looks the machine over and pulls the tine gear up. He doesn't even say thanks. Fucking asshole, I should have let the tiller eat him up. I go back in the house before he finishes and drives away with the tiller.

We were supposed to go to our nephew's wedding in Manitoba three days after the tilling accident, but I really don't feel up to it, so Rick goes by himself. Jo was coming to look after the farm while we were gone, and she still comes, delighted that I am in a position of reliance on her.

"What goes around comes around," she gleefully states. She's an awesome nurse. I don't even need to see the wounds, she cleans them up and rebandages them. The whole leg is a mass of colours: the bruises are yellow and orange and blue and even some green in there. I can't put any weight on it at all without extreme pain. I move around like a crab, dragging my behind upstairs to bed, one step at a time with my arms and the other leg. I use the same method to use the loo. I am not a good patient; I'm impatient. Jo brings *Sacagawea* and a whole bunch more fat books that keep me on the couch for days, and she treats me like a child. I eat it up.

The tiller doesn't come home for so long I start phoning. Everyone has been telling me I should sue the dealer, apparently even the dealer thinks I might. Since they have got my tiller back they've taken a video of how well it works with the tines on backwards. They have a piece of garden all worked up and they've sent a strong young man out to till with my tiller. A guy who was expecting the pull, working up soil that's already soft—it makes me furious. I think he is likely the one that put the tines on backwards. People who know them say they'll never admit any one of them did any wrong.

Should I sue them? I wonder. I phone a lawyer and tell him the story. He's a specialist in ICBC personal injury claims, and he agrees that I have a case, but he thinks it will be pretty costly to win against Honda. Costly is how he described it. He means money, but my time is pretty important to me too. Not simply the time it takes, but what the focus of that time would be. Courtrooms and lawyers and poor me, the victim. I borrow Jo's philosophy. "Hell," I tell her, "I'm not a Rototiller victim, I'm a survivor."

Jo tells me, "You know, people like that get it back. What they do, what all of us do, it all comes back. That's why a person has to be careful not to do something ugly that's going to bounce right back at them." Right on! The universe should be cooking up something special for that crew.

Leaky roof

I get a call from Newt saying he and Sadie are going to drop by and leave stuff here that Jo will pick up next time she's by. They know the way; sometimes they come to visit while Jo is house-sitting. Last time Jo was here she crazy-quilted a top on an old wool blanket and then she and Sadie beaded flowers and vines on top of the quilted side. The blanket weighs about six pounds and you could sleep outside in the winter time under it. The cat loves that blanket; she can't leave it alone. She nuzzles it and licks it, and leaves a coating of grey cat hair ornamenting it.

Newt drives in by himself. Usually he drives a big old Cadillac. He loves that car, and sometimes you'll see him parked in random places, sitting in his car beside the road, windows down and radio up, just watching the world go by. Some people are creeped out when they see him parked beside the road, thinking he's a weird guy. Today he's driving a little green car that looks brand new.

"What happened to the Caddy?" I ask.

"It's in the yard. This is a new car I bought for Sadie. We bought it yesterday and she drove it home. I'm giving it a tryout today."

"How do you like it?"

"It's okay, a bit gutless, but I'm used to my good car. This is a little shitbox, but it gets good mileage and it shouldn't break down. I had to get her a new car, the floor was rusted right out of the other one and you could always smell exhaust inside. I was worried Sadie would get asphyxiated just driving the seven miles into Fraser Lake."

"Where is she?"

"She's not feeling good today. We were in Prince all day yesterday getting this car and it tired her out. She tires out easy. And it's hard for her to get up your steps."

This I already know, the part about the steps. Jo was totally disgusted when she told me of the struggle Sadie had getting up the four steps leading to our door last time she was here.

Newt has a box of stuff that I put in the closet for Jo. "How is she, anyway?" he asks.

"Haven't you been talking to her?"

"Naw, Sadie's pissed because she thinks I phone Jo too much. And I can't say anything anyway because she's always listening."

"What do you mean?"

"I can't say anything personal."

"Well, you shouldn't be anyway!" I laugh.

"She's still the one I think about the most. She phoned me before; she wants some money."

"Did your mom pass away?" As soon as I've said it I'm embarrassed. I think of him and money and what comes to mind is his mother. Newt's mother has lived a very long life. She lost her licence because of a speeding ticket a few years ago and she was ninety-two then. Newt tells the story of his mom speeding—he says she was ninety-two going a hundred! And she was mad when they took her licence away. She must be at least ninety-five by now. My dad used to laugh about Newt waiting for the old lady to die so he could use up her money.

"Yeah, she passed away in the spring."

"I'm sorry to hear that." I say what I'm supposed to say, although I'm really not all that sorry to hear that a very old person passed away.

Newt must feel the same way because I can't see any trace of sorrow on his face. "She lived a good long life and died in her sleep. She didn't suffer."

"Are you the last one left?"

"No, I have a brother and a sister. They still live down at the coast. They got the lion's share." Newt pauses. "She lived with my brother at the end."

The little devil inside my head calls him a mercenary bugger, but outside I politely nod. He goes on: "I'd like to get something for Jo. Do you think she wants a car?"

"A car?"

"She wants some money. She says she's going to put in a new roof. But you never know with her."

"Have you been up there?"

"No. We keep saying we're going to, but so far we haven't." A thoughtful look passes over his face. "Now that we have the new car, maybe Sadie will want to make a run up there. I didn't like to take the old Caddy that far from home."

It's only a three-hour drive to get to Jo's doorstep from Newt's. The Caddy body is perfect, and Newt keeps it shiny. He has three other old cars in the yard for parts, so I assumed he tinkered with it a lot. Maybe not.

"The roof on her trailer leaks," I say.

"Yeah, she said." He looks uncomfortable "She wants money to fix it. She's not that good with money."

Newt visits for a couple hours; he knows our whole family and he asks about each in turn.

After he leaves I phone Jo, and she already knows his mother died and she sets me straight on the money thing. He isn't giving her money out of the goodness of his heart; he's giving her the money because he damn well owes it to her. She left after all those years with hardly anything, and that summer she'd given Newt all her savings, ten thousand dollars, to fix his Cat. The rollers and bearings had all needed changing. He'd promised her that he'd repay the money but never had. Until now she hadn't needed it, but now that she needs to replace her roof, she was calling the loan. And she wasn't asking for interest, just exactly what he owed her. Furthermore, she and Sadie had already had words about it. Sadie said, "Prove it!"

Newt's mother had an account book where she kept notes of her financial transactions, and every time Newt borrowed from her, which was apparently fairly frequently, she'd made a note in her book and deducted it from his inheritance. That's why his siblings got the "lion's share." We have a laugh over that tuned-in old lady. Good for her, trying to teach consequence till past her dying day—too bad Newt will never quite get it.

"Do you think he'll pay you?"

"He better! Give me a fucking car! What the—? Grrrr…"

"How are you going to do the roof?"

"Like a free-standing building. That's what I'd like. I'd like to be able to pull this trailer out from under it one day and build a straw bale house there. The roof is dripping pretty bad again; I think the tarp is getting too old. There are so many tires on the roof now that it's a big job just to change the tarp."

"Straw bale houses are very cool looking. Inside you can plaster them and you can build in benches and shapes."

"I know, and the window sills are so wide you could almost grow a garden in them!"

"Have roof, need house," I say and we laugh. "How are your hands?"

"Still not right. They're a lot better than they were, but I still can't get lids off jars, and if I try to cut kindling for starting the fire I suffer for doing it. I went to the doctor again and he thinks it's something to do with my elbows. I tell you I'm not getting any more operations. I'm done with the hack, hack. I'm going to learn how to deal with things the way they are."

"How the hell are you going to start your fires?"

"Oh, now I have the magic ingredients. I don't even need paper. I have a load of birch slabs; that's my kindling, two sticks and the fire is blazing. It's cold enough in the mornings now to light it every day, but by afternoon it's gotta be out."

Newt phones me once a month and assures me that he is going to give Jo money, but he never admits to me that he owes her. He says they talked it over (he and Sadie) and he needs to wait a little bit and he'll have the money ready. He says he's got the claim for the gold mine up for sale. That's surprising: he's always kept up his claim and always talks of what the price of gold is, gleefully when it's up, woefully when it's down, feeling richer or poorer from an item as ethereal as unclaimed gold in the ground. He must be justifying himself to Sadie. It's the one part of Newt that is Jo's alone, the time of the gold mining. The claim is more hers than his if you measure units of life force spent there.

Jo phones at random times. Good thing I'm up early, and I can think clearly already when she phones at 4:10 a.m. "Janet! The fucking roof has a new leak, and this time it's coming right out the light socket. There's four buckets sitting around this place 'plink, plink, plinking.'"

"Through the light socket?! That's dangerous! Have you got the breaker off?"

"No, I tried that. Then I have no power in the kitchen. I got the switch off."

"Holy shit, don't turn it on by accident."

"No fear of that, I taped the sucker down. I can't even do it by accident, nor can anyone else. Not that anyone else comes here. You know that young guy down the street, the one I made friends with in the summer? Well, he ain't coming in here ever again. The little squirt—he's young enough to be my son, younger than that even, and he made a pass at me. Yuck! His squirmy little lips, he thought he was going to have me. The nerve! What's he think—that I'm going to be his mother? My gate is closed to him, from now on. I'll talk to him if he passes on the street, that's all."

That makes me laugh. I met the guy when we dropped her off with the huckleberries. He is tall with long curly blond hair and nice white teeth in a friendly smiling face, maybe in his mid-twenties. He lives in South Town in a rental trailer and does odd jobs. Can't be too ambitious. Maybe he does need a mother.

"Come on—a little young stuff to curl up next to on those cold winter nights. Might be nice," I tease.

"Ain't never a night cold enough for that!"

Another day the phone rings at seven a.m. There is a note of panic in Jo's voice. "Phone me!" I call her back and she answers first ring. "I woke up and there was a noise like *bzzzt bzzzt* and crackling, and the lights blinked a bit and the breaker box is leaking. I shut it off."

"What do you mean, it's leaking?"

"Just exactly what I said. It's leaking."

"Leaking water?"

"What the hell else would it be leaking? I shut it off but now I'm sitting in the dark with a flashlight. At least the phone works."

"What are you going to do?"

"I'm phoning you. What should I do?"

I'm not really qualified to advise on this. What she should do is get a roof built over the whole thing, but that isn't really a helpful suggestion at the present time.

"Okay. Rip out the ceiling above it and see if you can divert the water away from there. There is still power above the box, so don't touch no wires. They should be insulated, but maybe not if they're wet. I'll call you back in twenty minutes."

I sit right by the phone for the whole twenty minutes, resisting the urge to call back. When I give in she answers right away, totally calm again. "That was the right thing to do. Now it's dripping four feet away. As soon as the box dries out I'll turn it on again."

"Have your valuables packed up by the door when you do," I advise.

Later that day I phone Newt and he answers the phone himself. Sadie has gone to visit her sister. He is free to talk about her and he does. He thinks she's lazy. It's the pot calling the kettle black, but I don't say that to him. I want to talk roofing.

"Have you been to Jo's yet?"

"No."

"Her roof is really bad; that place is leaking like a sieve. This morning there was water coming out the breaker box. She sure needs that roof."

"Sadie gets mad when I talk about it, but as soon as the gold claim sells, I'll pay her." There, he's finally said it: "pay" her, not "give" her.

"How easy is it to sell gold claims?"

"At the price of gold now, pretty easy. It makes the claim worth more and it'll be easy to sell."

"That's good, Newt, cause honestly, if Jo doesn't have a roof over that place pretty soon there won't be anything left but a big pile of mildew and tin."

"It's bad, eh?"

"Yeah, bad!"

"Sadie and Jo don't talk on the phone no more."

"How come?"

"I don't know. Sadie said Jo was sarcastic."

I can believe that, she is sarcastic, but sarcasm has its good side: it's a way to throw some funny into situations quite lacking in that attribute. I decide to grab the bull by the horns. "Does Sadie not want you to give Jo her money?"

The relief of not having to say it himself is evident in his voice. "You might say that."

"Well, I don't think you should let Sadie decide that. I can't think of what else Jo is going to do." I hope he can hear how disappointed that makes me.

I unburden myself on my husband. He offers to donate some timbers to the cause, but it isn't really fair to ask my husband to build my friend a roof. He says he was listening to CBC on his radio and they were talking about housing upgrades available through CMHC. That's Canada Mortgage and Housing Corporation. I check into it, and they give out money to bring older houses up to code and that includes wiring upgrades and roofing. I phone Jo and tell her about it.

Jo got married at fifteen when she was six months pregnant. The wedding was small and intimate; only the immediate families attended. The young family moved into an apartment in Smithers. It was the first time Jo had neighbours so close, and she made friends easily. By the end of two weeks she had friends in the building whom she had coffee and visits with after her husband went to work. She was so happy; she collected baby things and cooked and cleaned. She was proud of her husband: he was so smart and handsome too. He liked to come home to the clean house and the ready meal and for a while everything was perfect.

The chinks started showing up after a few months: the grilling during supper about where she'd been, who she'd been talking to, what she'd done all day. At first it was fun, telling him about her days. Then came the day when she felt defensive, didn't want to have to recount every instant of her day. Why she felt that way she couldn't really say: she'd done nothing wrong and told herself she was just being silly.

The birth of the baby changed things again. Her husband simply wasn't interested in the baby, not like she was. The tiny creature captivated Jo's heart. She couldn't understand why her husband didn't like the baby more, but it didn't matter so much, babies were more for mothers. She thought he'd like him better when the baby was big enough to do things. Her own body snapped back to shape in six weeks and her husband was interested in that. He wanted sex all the time, even when she was tired and wanted nothing to do with it. He didn't seem to care if she was in the mood; if he was, that was good enough for him. There came a night when she resisted, said she wasn't in the mood and could he please just go to sleep.

He went nuts. What followed was sex she didn't enjoy. He was rough and uncaring and after he was done he rolled over and went to sleep, seemingly unaware of the fatal blow he'd delivered to love.

The side of him that came out that night never went away. Jo thought maybe it was always there, held in check before by some barrier that had dissolved that night. He found that by being mean to the baby, he had control of the mother; she would do anything to protect her child.

Things deteriorated fast. At first Jo covered up the bruises and no one else knew. Then a new couple moved in downstairs. They had a small child that Jo spontaneously offered to watch while they packed their stuff in through the stairwell. She watched out the window until the truck was empty, and then brought the little boy downstairs to his new home. They had unpacked a coffeepot and Jo was having a quick cup with them when her husband came knocking on the door. He was home an hour early and Jo rose to greet him in surprise. He didn't stop to say hello, he just grabbed the baby off the table and Jo by the sleeve and marched them upstairs.

When they got to their own place, he didn't stop. He threw the baby at the couch and though he landed on the cushion and stayed there he started wailing at the top of his lungs. Jo couldn't run to him because she was being held by the hair as he yelled "whore" at her again and again. Jo had enough. There is an equalizer for every situation and Jo reached for one and put him out of commission. He was out long enough for her to phone the police and get an escort out of town. She and the baby went home to her dad's place.

A drop in the bucket

"Financial assistance programs are available for low income households, seniors, and persons with disabilities." That's what CMHC advertises on its website. That seems to fit the bill for Jo—she fits into two of the three categories and is closing in on the third. Maybe there are other avenues to getting money to fix her roof than Newt. She gets on it, starts by phoning them up and seeing what they can do. It looks like she can get somewhere between six and nine thousand. Surely that's enough for the roof.

Jo discusses her problem with the voice at CMHC. It offers to send a person out to assess the situation; they can do nothing till then. She agrees and two weeks later a young man knocks on the door and explains that he is working for CMHC. Jo is expecting him and lets him in. He has a clipboard with a form that he fills out as he goes. Jo wonders why he has to go through the house, it's a roof that she needs.

"Part of the process is to evaluate the home, and see what upgrades it needs to meet today's standards. My job is assessment, I look around to see what could be done and make a report. My report will go to another department and they will decide what needs to be done and make a budget for it."

Jo follows him around while he writes. He keeps a cheerful running commentary while he pokes at stuff, and pauses a long time at the electrical panel. "Hmmm, long time since I've seen this type of panel. It uses the old kind of fuses." He stops for a moment and addresses Jo. "Can you still buy these type of fuses?"

"I don't know, I have a bunch of spares. I never tried to buy them."

He pauses again at the taped light switch, raises his eyebrows, turns to Jo, and says, "Why?" She explains and he says, "Mm-hmm, mm-hmmm," and writes some more. The bathroom causes a lot more nasal talking and clipboard scribbling. He wants to know what happened to the hot water tank. There's just a hole in the wall that Jo has turned into a closet where the tank used to be. It quit working a while ago and Jo heats water on the stove. She explains it, feeling more and more like she has to justify how she lives to this young guy who has no idea of who she is, and resenting it exponentially each minute.

He spends a long time at the woodstoves and the uninsulated chimneys disappearing into the ceiling; he walks outside, goes back far enough to spot where they come out of the trailer and the addition. He writes more, comes back in, and looks in the living room where the roof is propped up. He goes close and pokes the end of his pen against the rafter showing through the plastic vapour barrier where it butts the new support. The soft wood gives under the pressure. Jo nearly cracks, and she's just about to tell him to go when he says he's finished and they'll get back to her in a week or two.

Jo doesn't slam the door behind him but she recognizes the impulse to do so. She feels like the man has violated her space with a negative judgement and it takes a while to calm down. She waters all the plants in the living room, talking to them while she does it. "You're happy here, aren't you? Look at your pretty blooms!" she says to them. Jo's read a book that has scientifically proven that plants have emotions, real feelings that can be measured. It was something she already knew, and there is a certain satisfaction in scientific proof being found for something a person has always known to be true but couldn't prove to anyone. Things like plant feelings or telepathy, or knowing the phone is going to ring just before it does. Thinking about these kinds of things is calming for Jo. She's learned to think deliberately, to turn her thoughts to the ones she enjoys thinking, and that is a skill worth knowing.

She strings a few lines of beads and hangs them on the curtain she's making. Her hands are getting more dexterous, although they still aren't strong and they still tend to seize up with painful cramps if she overdoes any repetitive motion. But, she's figured out the happy medium, when to change tasks. She spends some time quilting: this winter she's been making velvety textured tops, crazy-quilted on wool. There are so many fabrics now that look like velvet, mostly made into dresses. Jo bought a green garbage bag full of velvet dresses when the second-hand store had its "clearing out the old" sale and cut them up for quilting material. She's been making quilts for years and has developed her own style. She sews each piece right onto the wool blanket, using a big needle and big stitches. Then she takes a smaller needle and finishes the top side. She gathers the velvet in loose folds with the big stitches and when she's finished, the entire blanket top will be draped with soft folds of vibrant colour. She binds the edges with doubled-over layers of the same fabrics, scalloping them down the sides and at the foot. It's really heavy, the kind of blanket that makes you feel warm and safe when you crawl under it.

Maria phones and Jo is happy to hear from her. She sounds really good: she's enrolled in a welding course in Terrace, and it seems as though she really likes it. When she's done she'll be able to get a well paying job. The girls are doing okay in school; she's still having a little trouble with her younger girl, but she hasn't let them put her on medication. Her older girl is growing up. They are thinking about pressing charges against their dad. Maria says it's going to go to court, and Jo has mixed feelings about that. She knows from experience that conviction and jail time doesn't stop most child-rapists from re-offending. Jo asks her about the boyfriend, but Maria is evasive, says he's away right now, and yeah, everything's okay. Jo doesn't have to ask about the drinking. Maria brings it up herself. "You'll be happy to know I'm not drinking," she says. Jo snorts under her breath. She's heard that before, and it might mean she quit only a half hour ago, but out loud she encourages her. "Good for you!". Maria hangs up after promising to come and visit after the course is done and the kids get out of school. She frustrates Jo, overindulging in everything, but she is a true friend who calls just to say hello.

The neighbours have been getting friendlier. The couple next door are old, well, he's old and she's middle-aged. He'll probably outlive her though; she's a very large woman whose comfort zone doesn't extend much past her walls. The old man likes to go out walking and sometimes he walks with Jo. Often, afterwards they have a coffee together in the morning, the three of them sitting around the kitchen table. They're all concerned about the neighbourhood. People coming and going at all hours: don't those people ever sleep? They worry about theft and even Jo starts locking her door at night. The young guy down the street has a new girlfriend and yes, he was looking for a mother—this one is almost Jo's age. Maybe older, pretty funny.

It takes about three weeks for CMHC to send the papers to Jo. When she gets them she reads them over and over, trying to make sense of them. What she finds is that the roof is part of a package upgrade, but in order for them to do it, they want to bring everything up to code. This includes wiring, which may be a good thing, plumbing, another good thing, some structural upgrades and new insulation. But it isn't free. There is a free part, and they will give her a credit of six grand towards the total bill, which comes to thirty-two grand. Simply amazing. The whole place, land and all, is worth maybe half that much. And what would change? She'd still have a trailer built in the forties on a lot in South Hazelton, and she'd be carrying a mortgage that selling the place couldn't discharge. She kept the papers and reread them occasionally in the next days, and then she started the fire with them.

The love that the baby didn't get from Jo's husband flowed freely from her dad. If only love was enough! He was still drinking heavily and Jo couldn't leave the baby in his care; she didn't trust him to be careful enough. She knew she needed to get a job, to be independent. At this time, epilepsy was still striking her down at random. The first few times the world started firing in bursts she was able to sit down and wait it out, calm herself, send it off, but before long the seizures were racking her. She always managed to put the baby down before she passed out; dropping him was one of her greatest fears, passing out and dropping him.

He was growing fast, and he needed so much. Jo had a dozen cloth diapers that she was always washing, packing the water in from the creek and heating it up on the stove. There was a rack for drying above the stove and it was always full of diapers and baby clothes. He was a happy baby, willing to lie on a blanket and kick and goo at Jo while she worked around him. She was so anxious to start again, with the responsibility for the baby lying heavy on her shoulders. This precious little baby, he was hers to provide for. Though her dad never said a word about it, Jo knew she would have to get a job and start making a living for them. So far, her dad had bought all the canned milk and corn syrup and Pablum, had taken Jo to the second-hand store to get baby clothes, had brought a box of hand-me-downs from a friend, and had in general done all the providing. There were times when the clothing left on the step, the canned berries and salmon made a huge difference. Jo had dreams of a better life; she could hardly wait to get out of there, away from the drinking and the partying. Away from a dangerous man she still hated with a passion, who wanted her no less at sixteen with a baby than he did when she was eight. She no longer felt safe where she was. Even her husband knew where her dad lived, but she had no idea how to get away. Going to the welfare office was out of the question; her father would never let her. He hated welfare people. He said he wasn't prejudiced against anyone except for lazy people, and he said no one had the right to live off others just because they were lazy. She wasn't lazy; she wasn't a welfare bum.

Jo lived in this uneasy situation for months, months that felt like years. She did a few odd jobs, housecleaning and yard work. One night, when she had to dilute the milk so much it was almost water, the baby rebelled. He screamed and wiggled and wouldn't take the nipple. There were some cronies of her dad's hanging out there who wanted to know what was wrong. Jo explained that he didn't like the bottle because it was too weak, but it was the last can of milk so she couldn't fix it. The men dug around in their pockets and pooled their money, went to town and bought a whole case of milk. Jo was so grateful she couldn't even speak and her eyes filled with tears. The men understood. One gave her an awkward hug and told her to "hang in there." Underneath the gratitude was the internal question of where the next case of milk would come from. The baby was getting bigger and starting to move around. He wanted to be held all the time and he screamed every time Jo went out of his sight. She felt guilty for every minute she was away from him.

Then the thing happened that she was so scared would happen: she had a seizure that came on so suddenly it knocked her out. When she came to, the baby was under her. Her whole weight had been on him and he was screaming his lungs out. Jo kept feeling him over and over: he had a bump on his head, he cried louder when she felt his left arm, and he had bruises already coming up on his legs. Jo rocked him in her lap and cried along with him, feeling inadequate in every way. She sat there for hours, facing some hard truths, undisturbed by her father who was sleeping it off in the bedroom. She wasn't, she couldn't, be a good mother. No matter how hard she tried, she just kept hurting him. First it was her husband, now it was herself. She cried tears for herself and tears for her son, tears for her dad, tears for her marriage; she cried till she was empty.

Then she packed up a suitcase for her son and caught the next ride into town. She went to the social services office and tried to give them her son and his suitcase. She told them he needed a good family, that he deserved it. The lump on his forehead had turned black and blue. He looked like a battered child, and the lady at the desk who started to tell her that wasn't the way it was done was forestalled by another hard-eyed woman who picked up the baby, walked into another office, and returned with papers. She took down the information as she asked Jo questions: the baby's name, birthdate, parents. When they asked the father's name Jo was silent, and she never saw what the woman wrote down. When the woman asked if she wanted to put him up for adoption, Jo said yes, and then signed the paper that would take her son out of her life.

She stayed in town for a few hours, the enormity of what she'd done coming over her in waves. Though she thought she'd done the best thing she could have for the sake of the baby, she felt torn in two, felt much smaller without him. She caught a ride back home, but there was no sanctuary there. When her Dad found out what she'd done he was furious. He told her she was no daughter of his anymore and to get out. He roared off in the truck, and Jo found out later that he'd driven in a fury to social services to try to get the boy back, but it was too late, he was already gone. By the time he drove home, so was Jo.

Now you see it, now you don't

Jo phones and tells me the story of the CMHC offer to fix her house.

"That's not going to work for you," I say.

"No kidding. How much would I have to pay every month if I had a mortgage of twenty-six thousand dollars?"

"Depends on how long you take it over."

"Say ten years."

I get out the calculator and go 26000 divided by 120. "Two hundred sixteen a month principal, and you can probably double that because of the interest."

"How much is double that?" Jo talks in a little girl voice when she asks questions like this.

"About four hundred fifty."

"But Janet, interest is only a couple per cent, it can't be double."

"Yes it can. It's not straight 4 or 6 per cent, they figure it out for every year and add it all together; it's always like that."

"Well that's criminal. I might not be a math expert, but I know that's a hundred per cent interest, not four or six. How can they get away with that?"

"It's a monopoly," I assure her. "But what about the roof? Back to plan A? Are you even talking to Newt these days?"

"Yeah, he phones me when Sadie's not home. He's getting weirder, sometimes he talks like I just walked out the door last week. He wants to talk about all the things we did together, and he keeps saying his memory is getting bad, but that's all he does is remember things."

"Does he say anything about your money?"

"Oh yeah, he says he's selling the claim."

"Maybe he'll come through yet," I say, though I am not holding out much hope.

I am surprised when Newt drives in the very next day and even more surprised when he tells me he's come to give me a cheque for Jo. He walks in with the chequebook in his hand and has a coffee while he visits. He says he's giving me the money so I can pay for a roof for Jo. I must look surprised because he says, "If I send it to her, she might take a notion to go spend it on something else she doesn't need."

Inside I'm livid. He lived with Jo for years, and she left him with a suitcase of clothes in her hand, nothing else. She made a way for herself before she met him and has for the fifteen years since, and she can be trusted to look after her own money. What an asshole, I think, but outside I smile. What's the use of judging him now—he is what he is. He keeps repeating that he can't remember anything, all the while doing just as Jo says—remembering all kinds of things. It's annoying, like he's trying to pump sympathy from an empty tub. When he leaves he writes a cheque and hands it over. He says to make sure she uses it for the roof.

He's barely out of sight when I call Jo. "You won't believe it. Newt was just here and he left five grand for you!"

Jo starts screaming. "Whoo hoo! Half is better than nothing!" and yells some more happy in my ear, and I am pleased to be the bearer of such good news. I put Newt's cheque to me in the bank and send one to Jo. If she wonders why it's coming through me, she doesn't ask and I don't say.

... Gramma GreyGrouse

Jo says, "Some people don't need to be in your life very long before they influence you in ways that turn out to be important for the whole rest of your life. My Gramma is one of those people."

When Jo was sixteen she had some friends she could stay with, friends she meant to keep at arm's length. She knew one thing and that was plain: she needed to stay clear of love and men because nothing good had happened to her when it came to love or men. "Look at them, admire them, but don't let them get close," she thought to herself. The only man she trusted was her brother Sam and he was mixed up with a girl who was far too fond of drinking for Jo's liking. She didn't see much of them.

Her dad's girlfriend was part of the extended GreyGrouse family, and Jo had known some of them for years. They were unusual in that they owned property. They'd bought it and lots of people didn't like them on account of that. Jo had been at their home a lot. It was a bustling farmstead with animals and crops and she loved it there. Reigning supreme was Gramma GreyGrouse, the matriarch of the family, whom Jo had the greatest respect for. If Gramma said something that made it law.

There was a pit in the yard with ramps beside it that you could drive the car on, and climbing into the pit gave standing room under the car. It was the home of a nice guy named Dan. Little did she know then, but Dan would become a beloved brother. Back then he had a car and talked Jo into coming to the farm with him; he needed to change the oil. While he did that, Jo helped pick peas in the garden with the older women and the venerable Gramma GreyGrouse. The old woman showed her appreciation with a nod and a smile. "Nice to see you here, Jo. How you doing?"

"Doing good. I'm working part-time at the hotel." They worked throughout the afternoon, and Jo helped make supper. There was something almost holy about eating the things freshly harvested like that. Jo found herself opening up to Gramma, confiding her troubles, something she seldom did. "I need to find a place to stay though. I've been moving around, staying with friends."

"You come live here. You're a good girl, not lazy. You go back to school. You stay here and you go to school, you don't need to pay no rent." Gramma said it like it was an order.

"Really?"

"Young girl like you should finish school. What grade you have?"

"I passed everything in grade eight except math," Jo confessed.

"Could I really?"

"Go to town, get your stuff," Gramma ordered, and Jo found herself in a warm, welcoming home where she found the anchor she needed to rebuild some dreams. She became part of a functional family who welcomed her and treated her like a sister. Most of all they loved her, and she in turn liked being part of the family, they made her feel like one of them. Jo loved her new grandma. She was a fount of traditional wisdom and plant lore. When someone was sick, she always knew what plants to use. She taught Jo that yarrow stopped bleeding, that raspberry leaves would ease menstrual cramps, that smoke discouraged insects. It seemed as though she oozed information and Jo liked to follow her around and sponge it up.

It was by watching that family be a family that Jo figured out that the life she'd grown accustomed to simply wasn't normal. The dad was gone, but this family was tight, and everyone helped everyone. Jo didn't know how hurting she was till she got there, but somehow Gramma knew. Jo woke up more than once held firmly in her strong arms, being reassured, "Wake up Jo. It's all right. You're safe. Wake up, Jo." Till then, she never knew that she screamed with terror in the middle of the night, never before did she know how scared she was, and sometimes she felt that hurt leaving her in great gasping sobs. In the dark of the nights she was wrapped safe in the arms of a mother; it gave her a feeling of security that she'd never had before.

Going to school was a different story. She went back to grade nine lessons at sixteen, in a class with thirteen-year-olds who seemed worlds away. Math was still her downfall; merely opening the book sent her heart rate up and fogged her mind. After a while she stopped trying to do math, content to fail it. Social studies was all about European explorers discovering places in America, like the land was somehow lost—she thought memorizing the dates was stupid. Who the heck cared about that, and why wasn't there any history of Native people? Jo put social studies down as a waste of time and effort. If it wasn't for the worry of disappointing Gramma, who was so happy about her going to school, she'd have never made it through the first week.

Her epilepsy came back and knocked her down at random. Several times it happened at school, and the few who had tried to make friends with her didn't try anymore. Some of her new brothers and sisters were in school but none in her grade.

Months turned into years while Jo lived there. She quit going to school and got a job in town. It was a happy period in her life and passed all too quickly. Once, she moved out in a fit of pique. It started as an argument; she can't remember why it started, but the part that sticks was that one of her new sisters accused her of sleeping with one of her new brothers to get in the family. She said Jo used the family, coming when it was convenient and going back to her dad's when that suited her. Jo was outraged: other people slept their way into situations but she'd never done that. Especially not with her brother! She wouldn't stay one more second in a house where she wasn't welcome; she packed her bags and headed out the door. She had a friend downtown, Jamie, who was renting a small one-bedroom apartment and Jo went there. Jamie had one small boy and was expecting again. Her husband had a camp job and she was lonely. Her family didn't visit and she welcomed Jo's company. Jo helped her with the little boy and assuaged some of her loneliness for her own son.

Jo had a job at the Bulkley hotel, waitressing. They gave her four hours a day weekdays at a dollar fifty an hour, tips on top. It was nice to have regular money. The tips she took home every day, sometimes more in tips than she made hourly. She didn't mind sleeping on the tiny couch in Jamie's apartment. The seizures she had were all when she was at home, but often they left her with a complete blank for numbers and at work she wasn't able to figure out change for the customers or add up the bill. Luckily one of the other waitresses was a math whiz and didn't mind doing Jo's. She didn't act all superior about it, either. Jo cleaned her tables sometimes to make up for it.

She had been at Jamie's for ten days when one morning she met Gramma GreyGrouse in the lobby of the hotel. It was very unusual for the old woman to come to town; usually she sent people to get what she wanted, and she obviously was looking for Jo who was delighted to see her. The old eyes searched Jo's face. Gramma nodded to herself, and asked only, "Where're you sleeping?"

"At Jamie's. She's got a couch."

"You come home."

"Not everybody wants me there." Jo tried to sound as if she didn't care.

"I want you, you come home. This is the third time I come looking, you come home." Jo nodded. A person didn't argue with Gramma. Especially since she had made three trips to tell her. Jo couldn't recall a time when the old woman went to town three times in ten days.

Going home again was nice, and it was certainly nice to know she was important enough for the old woman to search her out, to take the trouble to go looking for her. Gramma did want her, and so did almost all the family. Jo felt an exception in the sister she'd quarreled with. The apology had been wooden and her sister's eyes hadn't agreed with her lips. They had no more fights, but a chill set in, the kind of chill that can last decades.

The only thing that was missing in Jo's life was her son, and whenever she thought of him she hurt. She missed him so much. Once she'd gone back to the social services office when the urge to know became too strong to deny but they wouldn't tell her who had him or where he was—they said she didn't have any right to know. Tears had welled up in her eyes right in front of the lady at the counter, and while tears didn't float any sympathy out of that hard heart, the lady at the other desk had a softer one; she rose and left when Jo did, holding the door for her. In the hallway she touched Jo on the arm to stop her. Jo looked up, embarrassed by her wet eyes, but the woman gave her a sympathetic look and spoke very quietly. "I'm not supposed to tell you this but I want you to know your boy went to a good family, a nice couple. They live down south and have a beautiful home. I know they wanted a son very, very much. He's going to be all right."

"Do you know if they changed his name?" Jo wanted him to still have his name. She desperately hoped no one would change it. "I don't think so," the woman dropped her eyes, gave her arm another squeeze, and hurried away. Jo gained the street, hurried around the corner, and made for the park. She collapsed there under a tree and sobbed great heaving sobs. It was so final—he was really gone. Until then it had seemed surreal. Sometimes she'd see someone with a baby and hurry up to see if maybe it was hers, looking away and feeling foolish each time her anxious eyes beheld a stranger. When she heard a baby cry, she would start, then remind herself he was gone. She jiggled her groceries at the checkout counter if she even saw a baby in the line-up. Sometimes in a car driving by streets full of houses she'd wonder if behind one of those curtains her son was playing on the floor or maybe sitting up. He was starting to sit up good when….oh God, it was so hard. She'd probably never see him again. He was gone as sure as yesterday. She stayed on the ground, arms wrapped around her knees, forehead resting on them while she cried her heart out. If anyone saw her and thought it was odd to see a beautiful young girl so distressed, no one stopped to help.

I have eight brothers and sisters. We are all married and most have grown children—together we are a formidable work force, and I picture a work bee at Jo's house. We have some six by six beams from a shed that we're tearing down and a trailer to haul them and I phone Jo and tell her my plan, to have everyone come and spend a weekend there to build her a roof. I tell her she needs to have someone come and put concrete in Sono tubes for a foundation, so we don't have to waste a day on cement. She nips my idea in the bud.

"No friggin' way. That many people all at once? Can't we just do it ourselves, you and Rick and me?"

"If we had two weeks, maybe. It's a big job. If everyone comes we could maybe get it close to finished on a weekend, but there's no way three people could, and no disrespect but you're kind of useless for hammering nails or doing heavy stuff. Those beams themselves are heavy when you're trying to stand them on end."

"Well, we have to think of something else then, because I can't even imagine all you people here. No disrespect yourself, but I don't think even a new roof is worth having that much company at once."

We both laugh. Jo has an aversion to crowds. She hasn't been to a family function for a long time, and there is no hiding that she avoids us en masse. When she's here visiting, it's hard to talk her into going to the Legion in Fraser Lake where the guys sometimes get together to play and sing. She always wants to know ahead of time who's coming, which is a little difficult to say since it is a bar. It's usually safe to say "no one," also easier to coax her out. When she does come, she has a good time and sometimes a great time. Lots of people remember her from when she lived with Newt, and she's got many more friends than she knows.

"Well, that was my idea shot to hell. You got another one?"

"Give me a couple weeks. I have some people up here. I know this guy, he's a friend of my cousin's, he's a carpenter and usually does big jobs, but maybe he can do it. How much do you think it should cost?"

"It'll cost all of it, maybe more if you have to pay labour."

"Can you do me a big favour? Find out how much the tin will cost? Just silver tin, nothing fancy."

"Okay. How long is the trailer?"

"I don't know. I think it's forty, maybe forty-eight feet. And it has to be wide enough to cover the joy-shack."

"How wide is it?"

"I don't know, eight feet, maybe ten. Close."

"Close doesn't work when you're measuring for tin. How about you go measure and I'll call you back in a few minutes."

"I don't have a measuring tape."

"Not even one of those cloth ones for sewing?"

"No, I hate trying to read them. I hate all those lines. I measure things by using string, I stretch out a string and then I use that length."

It's the self-professed fetal alcohol raising its head; fractions belong with algebra in Jo's head. She hangs up after saying maybe her neighbour will measure it for her and write it down. Jo says she's got fetal alcohol when it comes to her math skills. She thinks there is a mathematical comprehension hole in her brain. She could never be a cashier who had to count out change. She certainly has some kind of block: hardly anyone has to struggle with numbers so much. The co-op and the building supply store give exactly the same quote for the tin by the square foot. Ordering trim to go around almost doubles the cost.

Jo doesn't need to measure because the carpenter came by to look at the job, and she's happy to report he'll do it. He told her he thinks he can get it done for right around her five grand, give or take a little. She doesn't know when he'll get to it, but he's promised she won't go through another winter with the roof leaking. That's good news and a welcome relief to my overworked husband—something that disappears off the "to do" list without the effort of doing is a good thing.

Oblate apology

The most sincere sounding apology is the one proffered by the Missionary Oblates of Mary Immaculate. It was authored by Reverend Doug Crosby OMI in 1991, as President of the Oblate Conference of Canada on behalf of the Missionaries Oblates of Mary Immaculate living and ministering in Canada. In it, he apologizes for "how deep, unchallenged, and damaging was the naive cultural, ethnic, linguistic, and religious superiority complex of Christian Europe when its people met and interrelated with the aboriginal peoples of North America."

He goes on to say, "We apologize for the part we played in the cultural, ethnic, linguistic, and religious imperialism that was part of the mentality with which the peoples of Europe first met the aboriginal peoples and which consistently has lurked behind the way the Native peoples of Canada have been treated by civil governments and by the churches. We were, naively, part of this mentality and were, in fact, often a key player in its implementation. We recognize that this mentality has, from the beginning, and ever since, continually threatened the cultural, linguistic, and religious traditions of the Native peoples."

There is an underlined sentence, the only one in the document, that states that they apologize for the *"existence of the schools themselves,"* recognizing that the biggest abuse was not what happened in the schools, but that the schools themselves happened. There is another paragraph that apologizes in a particular way for the personal abuses that happened in the schools and they wished to publicly "acknowledge that they were inexcusable, intolerable, and a betrayal of trust in one of its most serious forms."

If everyone in Canada felt the way this group feels then there would be an end to government claims of Native lands. The Natives were here first, no one is disputing that. They already owned the land by inherent right, and colonial powers simply confiscated it. A modern weighing of right and wrong has to admit the wrongness of the Doctrine of Discovery. What if the apologies were nationwide and heartfelt? What if every person, as the Anglicans said, bears the blame for this and we decided to make it right? What would we do? Give all the Crown land back? Make new rules for resources, based on the rules that the Natives hold sacred? What that would look like?

Fixing the roof?

Jo's contractor comes and builds the roof in late summer. He sets the beams on end on cement pads, makes a simple truss roof out of two by six, straps it, and screws down the tin. He extends the metal stovepipes so that they reach out through the new roof and flashes around them. The whole job from start to finish only takes a couple weeks, and Jo is some happy when they're done. The cost is twelve hundred more dollars than what she'd budgeted, but the man says "no problem" and she can pay him when she can afford it. That sure is nice, and Jo is very grateful.

She is on long-term disability now, and the nine hundred a month is almost enough money for her. She's lived on far less. Sam has been laid off from his job and is broke most the time, and she's able to help Sam out once in a while with a little cash infusion. She orders wood for the winter, compost for the garden, and more hay bales for the yard. Last year's bales are disintegrating fast: the worms are crazy big and busy. The bales are half the size they were when she put them there. The one she perched in the middle of the good soil is already soil and it gives her vast satisfaction to know the worms and the earth are doing all the work. She gets eight bales this time and two dump truck loads of compost. Now the neighbours aren't quite so hostile. The old guy comes over and asks if she minds selling him a few wheelbarrows of the compost. He thinks maybe it would do his garden good to top-dress it. Jo's heart overflows, that he who looked down on her and talked crap about her last year is now being her friend and acknowledging that she knows some things too. "I will give you as much as you need, just help yourself," she offers with sincerity and he does, covering his postage stamp garden with a generous layer.

Jo takes out the insulation in three places and replaces it with new, stapling a new vapour barrier up and taping it to the old with Tuck Tape. It feels so much snugger, warm and tight. The psychological strain of worry is gone too, and Jo feels full of life, that somehow she's paid her dues and now the universe is providing her with comfort and abundance. She wishes everyone in the world would focus on being grateful instead of whining about everything. Most of the people she visits are whiners: they are happy to tell her about what's wrong with them, with the world, with the weather. So many people seem to be in self-inflicted pain, lacking a proper sense of humour. In fact, she finds that quite a lot of people are depressing to be around. She tries to limit her exposure to those people.

For a long time she's had no long-distance privileges on her telephone. She buys long-distance minutes, and when they're used up they're gone, so there's never a crazy phone bill coming in later. She decides to get caller ID, so she knows who is calling before she answers, then she can't be politely trapped on the phone by someone she doesn't even want to talk to. She's got friends that she hangs out with. One is the old lady she gets her hay and firewood from whose husband has passed over; she's got lots of kids, married with children grown, but none of them seem to be really close to their mom, not to the point of hanging out with her, and Jo is more than happy for her friendship. The elder is still spry. She's been a country woman all her life and is full of lore. She's got a wonderful sense of humour and Jo admires her immensely. Another is her Filipina friend whose focus is food, but she also gardens and she and Jo have a lot in common. Another friend she's not so sure of—she's the wife of an old friend of Jo's and Jo puts up with a lot from her because she's married to her good friend. This woman is fun but terribly bossy. It takes all Jo's self-control not to tell her off sometimes; especially when she gives advice like it's an order to perform better. "You need to get your hot water tank fixed," she tells Jo, her order reinforced with a hard-eyed look.

"I don't mind heating it on the stove."

"Packing water isn't good for your hands."

"I pack it over in small amounts, it's good exercise."

"You shouldn't!" she turns to her husband. "Tell her she should get the hot water tank fixed."

He smiles indulgently at her. "I don't tell Jo what to do," he says, but she doesn't understand what he's telling her and every time she sees Jo she reminds her to do it.

Jo doesn't tell her that the stove is her answer to on demand heat. She doesn't tell her that her power bill is only ten dollars a month because she hardly uses electricity—it's a deliberate choice, not an accident—and that the reason she doesn't have a hot water tank is because she doesn't want one. She doesn't feel she should have to justify her choices to anyone and on that note she won't explain it. She tries to avoid this friend after a while and is happy she has caller ID.

... Moving on

At eighteen, Jo was engaged to be married again. She'd known Jon for years, and it was a case of friendship turning into love; when he asked if she'd marry him it was easy to say yes. Her resolution to stay away from men and love had flown out the window. It was a fun summer; the seizures had receded into memory and Jo was happy. She and Jon spent a lot of time with her father. Their relationship had slowly repaired itself, but these days her dad didn't seem his normal self although he claimed nothing was wrong. He coughed a lot and drank mostly wine because whiskey made him sick.

Neither Jon nor Jo was old enough to buy liquor; the drinking age was still twenty-one. Usually they could get a bottle from Jo's dad, or if push came to shove the cook at the hotel would buy it for them. Jo didn't like to drink much, a few drinks to be social, and she seldom drank enough to be drunk. Sometimes Jon would drink a lot but mostly he was like her, nursing a drink for hours.

They had fun together and sex was something Jo learned to look forward to. They had sex in the car, sex in bed, sex in the woods, all naked in front of nature. Except for the first couple months of her marriage, sex had been an unpleasant experience for Jo, but Jon taught her to appreciate sex for the fun and exuberance of it. She was in love, and her determination to admire men from a distance stayed off in the distance.

Jon was good friends with her brother Dan, and there was a whole crowd of peripheral friends that big families attract. Some of them were older, able to go in the bar, and often Jo saw them in the restaurant where she worked. She began to have a wide circle of acquaintances. Between her and Jon, they knew most the citizens of Telkwa and half of Smithers. Jo was happier than she'd been for a long time, and though sometimes she longed for news of her son, she never talked about it to anyone, it was a taboo subject. Jo had stayed a couple weeks at Jamie's when the new baby girl was born, and it had all came back to her when she helped care for the tiny infant. She missed her son again with all her heart and soul. Sometimes she tried to send a wave of love on the wind to him, hoping he'd get it, somehow, somewhere.

For one reason or another, Jon and Jo kept postponing the date for the wedding. They'd set the date for the third time. "Three times lucky!" Jon had said.

This particular night Jon and Jo stopped at the hotel to pick up some smokes. Jon sat in the car and Jo went in. She visited with some friends in the lobby while they all waited for the clerk to finish with another customer. It took some time, and when she got back to the car Jon was furious. "What were you doing in there so long with Simpson? I saw him come out. Was he talking to you?" Jo nodded, and said, "Yeah, we were talking."

"About bloody what?" Jon yelled. "Look at me! Tell me why my woman is in the store for a fucking half hour chatting up goddamn Simpson?" The fight was on, she protesting her innocence and him trying to convince her she'd done something wrong. Suddenly Jo saw in Jon the same thing she'd seen in her first husband, the jealous, angry streak that had led to so much violence and hurt. Her resolution came back and she stared at Jon in silence. She said nothing more to exonerate herself. She'd done nothing wrong and she had enough of jealousy. The rest of that life, that possibility, crumpled into ruins. The next day she got on the bus for Williams Lake, going down to visit Jon's sister for a bit. She left her ring with Dan to give back to Jon.

Newt starts failing

I see Newt in Vanderhoof. The occasion is my uncle's funeral. Uncle was a favourite of mine, my father's oldest brother, the one who first moved out to BC from the prairies and wrote the family telling them of the fruit trees that grew at the coast, the mild winters, the grace of Vancouver. He died at ninety-two, remaining alert and interesting all his life. His family asks me to do the eulogy. We don't have religion but we're all pretty sure of an afterlife, and I'm as close as our generation comes to being a public person.

At the door of every public event there is a cluster of smokers. In Canada—maybe not in the whole country but for sure in BC—the smokers have to stand at least nine feet from the door. That's how crazy it's become; we actually have to have a law about such dumb shit. Anyway, this day Newt is standing on the steps with his cigarette, right at the doorway. He looks saggy, as though his skin has grown suddenly too big for him to fill. He's got no colour at all, but he's dressed neatly; his hair is thin but it's still there, kind of wavy, nicotine yellow, still a bit long.

"Hi Norinne," he says to me. He's looking right at me and holding out his hand for a squeeze. I nod back. "Hi, Newt." I don't care what name he calls me.

"Your name is Norinne?" he says, giving me a hard look. I nod again; it's as though he's doing it deliberately, like when he says he can't remember; I wonder if he's really losing his grip on the world or if he's pretending. I don't have enough attention left this day to focus much of it on him, so I escape indoors.

My uncle was an incredible man and the hall is full of people, filling the chairs and standing along the walls. I tell stories from his life, we laugh about some of the things he did that have become family tales, I imitate him—talk how he'd talk and cuss how he'd cuss and make everyone laugh. It's easy to do the eulogy for an old person. They have lived the maximum time span allotted and I simply can't be too sad that they died. I don't believe death is an absolute ending, I believe it's a doorway and often a blessed relief. I believe the spirit of the person is many times attending their own funeral, and I try to make sure Uncle knows how much we all loved him.

I don't see Newt again that day but the rest of my family all talks to him, then we talk about him when we're together and everyone agrees that he's losing it. I call Jo and she says it's no wonder it's happening, he's been hypnotizing himself to stop remembering for a whole year already.

"The old thought, word, action! Think it, say it, then do it!"

"Careful what your lips say." Jo starts giggling "Careful what your brain thinks!"

"At least don't say bad things about yourself, and don't give yourself such bad suggestions. Imagine saying to yourself that you can't remember anything! It would have been so much better if he had a big enough ego to say 'I remember everything', even if he didn't. That way at least he'd have had a chance.

"Sadie's mean to him. They're mean to each other; they don't talk nice or be nice to each other. Their house is abusive, doubly abusive," Jo says.

"I saw him earlier this summer, sitting in his car down by Swan Park, at the turn by the railway tracks where the pullout is," I say. "He was parked there with the window down and the radio on and I thought it was probably him. I was staring and he saw it was me and waved, but I didn't stop."

"Yeah, he spends a lot of time in his car, sitting and listening to music. Most afternoons and evenings he goes to the pub in Endako. However, they deserve each other. If I ever feel sorry for him, which doesn't happen too often, I remind myself that he's lying in the bed he made for himself."

"It's one of those instances where the universe is giving him exactly what he's owed," I agree, and she tells me a story about how one day Newt was sitting in his car in Endako in plain sight of the local crack house. He'd apparently been sitting there one too many times and had made the regulars nervous. He got pulled from his car, roughed up, and warned to quit sitting there. Endako is a little town and they knew him, and he knew them, and even though he really was no threat to them at all, he took the warning and started parking elsewhere.

I tell Jo of the upbraiding I got after my uncle's funeral from an older Portuguese neighbour. He's lived in Canada for most of his life, but he and his wife remain Portuguese and they are devout Catholics.

He cornered me in the grocery store after the funeral and got right in my face. He emphasized his words by jabbing his finger in my shoulder as he lectured.

"There are two things you should not do at a funeral; one is laughing and one is swearing. There is no respect for the dead when you are laughing and swearing." I don't take criticism well, and especially not from someone who I barely respect to start off with. I asked him if he thought he was going to heaven when he died and he acknowledged that he likely would. "I'll see you there, and we'll talk about this again." I told him and brushed past, totally pissed off.

Jo tells me to ignore the old buzzard, that there are millions of people like him who think their way is the only way and that's mostly what is wrong with the world: the intolerance of people towards those who don't share their beliefs.

I agree with her and say I'm going to let it go. Well, maybe not let it go so much as file it away, label it "bad press."

Jo was almost nineteen when she left Jon. She headed to Williams Lake where one of Jon's sisters lived and got a job right away, detailing the cars for the police department. She liked the feeling of being on the other side; before she knew any Mounties personally, she'd put them in one category: the enemy. Never, except in one, long-ago incident, had the cops ever seemed like the good guys. Now, to her surprise, there were a few of them she liked. Her stereotypical image of a policeman was someone with a power-tripping personality and a magnified sense of his own self-worth. Now she was meeting nice cops, however, it was easy to keep her distance from these men; she knew she wouldn't like to be around them full-time. They sure have a rotten job, focusing on everything that's wrong. Jo worked there just long enough to save enough money to buy a car to roam around in, and then she roamed around. She felt free and independent, and she liked driving to new places and seeing new things.

When she was broke, she'd stay in one place for a while and get jobs cleaning or waitressing. She liked the cleaning jobs best, but waitressing paid better. At one point, she went to visit Jamie who'd moved down to the coast so her husband could get a job where he was home at night. They had a nice place rented in Surrey, and they showed her around Vancouver. To her, the city seemed like an anthill, with people scurrying every which way. At night, the orderly rows of car lights sweeping the walls seemed like so many ants off to do endless tasks, forever circling their circuits of concrete. Jo liked visiting Vancouver, but she liked it better when the bustle faded out in the grandeur of the Fraser Canyon, heading north on Highway 97.

Things didn't go well for Jamie and her husband in the city. He ended up with a broken leg from an accident unrelated to work, and since he didn't have any insurance to cover him while he recovered, they weren't able to make ends meet. One of Jo's visits was at that exact time. She knew about the accident, but not the money crunch—that became evident when she arrived. There weren't a whole lot of extras in the cupboard, and in her friends' eyes she read anxiety. Jo was flush, and ever generous, and it was easy for her to convince them to let her help. She "rented" the couch in their apartment and got a job at King George Highway poultry farm. The man at the interview asked how she was with first aid, and she told him she had a ticket, so she was listed as first aid help. He was pleased about her first aid ticket, explaining that though there were very seldom injuries on the job site, there were hundreds of workers and occasionally someone would cut themself. The only other first aid person was himself. Jo thought to herself that she could bandage cuts with the best of them, and at the first aid course they had taught her to administer CPR and mouth-to-mouth so she was confident enough to take on the position.

The kids were the best part of staying with Jamie. Jo would wake up to little faces with big eyes peering at couch level into her own. So sweet! She liked to take the kids for walks after work, stroller pulled behind till the short ones were tired, and then letting the boy ride on the back with his little sister in the seat. On the weekends and on payday, they'd go shopping. Jo supported them till the broken leg was healed and then stayed on for a while when the man it was attached to walked out the door and didn't come back.

One of the jobs at the poultry farm was cleaning bins. They were hard plastic, with lids that folded down, and they were washed, dried and stacked, and then carried to the storage room. Jo had done the job for weeks, and one day she stepped through the door, backing into it to open it with her butt and pivoting on her heel to fit the tubs through. The foot landed on something that moved, and her whole weight—with the stack of tubs on top—came crashing down on a wheeled cart for transporting pallets, made out of angle iron. She landed doing the splits, spread-eagled right on top of the rails; it was pure and instant agony. After heaving off the tubs, she rolled on the ground for a while. She tried to get to her feet but couldn't, so she crawled to a low bench and leaned over it, moaning. Two other workers arrived, and when she said she'd fallen on the cart, they started wondering out loud who might have left the cart there. They wondered if they should call the ambulance, but Jo refused. She just wanted to go home. The owner took her there himself and helped Jo hobble into the house. She ignored everyone who wanted to help her and all of their offers to take her to a doctor. Finally Jamie's brother told Jo, "If you don't show me I'm going to put you in the car and take you to a doctor and he's going to look." So Jo swallowed every bit of modesty and showed him her crotch. She joked to him that he was the first person to see it since Jon, and he laughed, then became sober-faced when he had a look at the black and blue that was spreading all down the tops of her thighs. He told her what it looked like. "You might have broken blood vessels or something."

"Well, it's sure as hell nothing a doctor could fix anyway. You want to do something? Go get me a sack of burdock leaves, that's what I need." When the leaves arrived, Jo soaked them in warm water and folded them inside a piece of cheesecloth to make a big pad which she packed around her sore bottom and changed frequently. After three days, the swelling went down but the black and blue persisted for weeks. The culprit who'd left the cart in the doorway was gone when she went back to work, but ever after Jo couldn't walk through that doorway without looking first. She was tired of doing that job anyway.

For a couple of years, whenever I phoned Jo we always had some conversation about the leaking roof, and we're both smug about it now. I still ask, "And how is your roof?" and she always says, "It's very good," and we have little self-satisfied chuckles over our words.

This particular day has been one of those fall days that take your breath away. It's the second day of hard frost and the first one has left the trees brilliant shades of yellow, red, and gold. There is a sparkling coating of frost over everything and when the sun bursts over the horizon it turns the world into glittering gold. When I phone Jo I am full of the morning sunrise and it isn't till I ask how her roof is that I notice she's unusually subdued. "It's Fucking Leaking," she says in a tiny, well-modulated snarl.

"You're joking!"

"*Not!*"

"How? How can it leak? It's solid, covered by tin. It can't leak."

"I am telling you it's leaking whether you want to believe it or not. There is a bucket half full by the stove and another one in the kitchen. It ain't pretend water."

"But it rained and rained in early September and it didn't leak then. How can it leak now?"

"*Janet!*" she yells in my ear. I am quiet for a second, then ask, "Is it freezing there?"

"Yeah, it did last night."

"Is it thawing out now?"

"Barely. The sun's not hitting full on yet. How is it there?" Her voice is full of controlled politeness.

"It must be condensation; there must be frost building up at night. That could be why. Hey, phone that guy and tell him."

Her voice gets even tighter. "I left a message for him last time it leaked and he hasn't got around to answering it yet. I tried to phone him a few times, but funny thing, he never seems to answer when I call."

"Maybe he's really busy. What do you mean 'last time it leaked'? How come you never said anything before?"

"I didn't want to tell you."

The roof saga continues. Another opinion is that there was no tarpaper or membrane installed under the tin, so the heat escaping from the trailer roof might be building up condensation on the bottom side of the tin, and it will only leak while the weather is frosty at night and thawing during the day. There are about six weeks in the spring and another six in the fall where we can get that kind of weather. Twelve weeks in all. She now has a three-season roof, but she can't think of what to do about it and neither can I. At least there are only two drips and they're localized, Jo will be happy when it freezes up for the winter. She pulls out the soggy insulation from those two spots, which she thinks might make it build up quicker and leak even more, but the improvement in the air quality demands it. Jo begins to refer to the drips as the automatic humidifying system. She decides to get someone to unscrew the tin next summer, install the membrane, and screw it back on. It simply can't be that big a job.

Beginnings and endings

Jo moved up to Endako when she was twenty-three. Her brother Dan moved there from Hazelton. He'd split up with his girlfriend and moved to Endako, getting a job in the molybdenum mine. Jo stopped in to see him on her way up north. She'd grown tired of the city, and Jamie was making out all right, so it felt like a good time to go. Jo's resolution to stay away from men was holding strong and she wanted to be back in the north, away from the bustle of the city. There weren't many houses for rent in Endako, but Dan found a small one that he'd described to Jo as "not bad." When she arrived, she saw that he had overstated it. Her dad would have described it as a tarpaper shack. Dan urged her to stay for a while and she didn't hesitate to agree; Dan was her favourite brother after Sam. Sam still occupied a special place in her heart; she would still do anything she could to help Sam. Dan was in a different category; he never seemed to need any help—he was fun and flirty and they could talk for hours. He was easy to be around and Jo didn't care about the tiny shack, didn't care that there wasn't an indoor toilet; there was a good outhouse out back, and the kitchen sink had running water and an outdoor drain. Jo accepted these things as part of northern living.

When she decided to stay, Jo went to the hotel, asked if they needed help, and got a job the first day. She'd been working there for a couple months when she first saw Newt. He was the kind of guy who caught your eye. Tall and handsome with almost flashy good looks, he had blond curly hair and bright blue eyes in a smooth shaven, angular face. He was wearing a T-shirt tucked into jeans and was tanned to a glowing bronze. Jo noticed the hair on his arms was so golden that it almost glowed in the dim light of the bar. He looked her in the eye when she came to the table to serve him, and then his gaze swept down and up her, grinning as his eyes swept back up. He pursed his lips in a little whistle. "Well, lookee here—where did you come from, Beautiful?"

Jo grinned back; she could flirt with the best of them. "I live here."

"I live here too, I've never seen you before."

"I just moved here."

"Endako just turned into a better town," he said, and his smile tugged her resolution a bit off kilter. "Bring me Grand Marnier by itself and a beer."

Jo grinned back. Grand Marnier—hardly anyone drank that—strange request! She brought him his order and he tipped her the same amount as his tab. She nodded thanks and tucked it in her pocket. Newt stayed till closing time, talking to her when she wasn't busy and moving to a stool by the bar while she wiped the glasses and tidied up. He was a generous tipper, and he talked non-stop in between tiny sips of his liqueur, swishing it around in his mouth before swallowing. Jo didn't know how he could drink Grand Marnier by itself: she found it sickeningly sweet and she shuddered when she saw him swallow. By the time the bar closed that night she knew some things about him: he'd just returned home from a trip down to Ladner where his parents lived; they were loaded; and he owned a home just outside of town on a little acreage. She'd made a new friend. Briefly, she wondered if he was married. There wasn't any ring on his finger, but that wasn't necessarily such a good clue, most men didn't wear them anyway. He hadn't mentioned a wife and made it sound like he lived alone. She pushed thoughts of him away. It didn't matter to her anyway, because she was sworn off men getting any closer than her elbow.

Jo and Dan got along great, and there was always laughter in their small home. Dan's job at the mine paid well, but not as well as the workers wanted; there was constant talk of strike and Dan didn't know how long the work was going to last. He went day by day; so far, so good. Dan often came to the bar after work, and soon he and

Newt were friends. Newt invited both Dan and Jo to supper and he cooked it himself, plain food: potatoes, carrots, and steak. The house was obviously new, and Newt said he'd mostly built it himself. Jo's dad would have approved of the snug little house; it was plumbed throughout, with a wood cookstove in the kitchen and a cast iron heater in the living room. It was cozy and warm and occupied by an old dog who laid his head on Jo's lap throughout the meal. After eating, Jo cleared the table and washed up the dishes in the sink, followed by the dog who patiently waited while she tidied, then once again laid his head on her lap when she sat down on the couch.

"Looks like you've captivated my dog," Newt noted.

"All dogs like me."

"I can see why," he grinned. "If I was that dog I'd be humping your leg already."

Dan and Jo laughed along with him. Since the day Newt met Jo he'd been flirting outrageously, and she was used to it. She liked him. He was older than she was but he was interesting; he talked about books and gave his opinions. He lent Jo some of his favourites, introduced her to Ayn Rand, and spent hours dissecting her work. Jo admired his thinking.

Newt was working that summer, clearing land. He owned a Caterpillar crawler, a big, iron-tracked machine with a blade on the front. He called it the Cat and told Dan, "I cleared off the site for that mine you're working at, me and my friend. We both had Cats. We worked in tandem; there used to be a hump where that hole you're working in is."

Newt would get off work and come for supper in the hotel, which had a restaurant beside the bar. Patrons could order supper from the restaurant and eat in the bar. Newt would stay in the bar till closing time, and then give Jo a ride for the two blocks home. After his job ended, he was in the bar every time Jo worked, the whole shift. He told her stories about the people that came in; he'd been in Endako for a while and knew most of the patrons. She and Dan became regular visitors to his home, and when the mine went on strike and Dan moved away, Jo took up Newt's offer of a room in his house. She knew what that meant: the offer was more than a room, she was moving into a new relationship, her resolution tucked into a tiny corner of her mind, forgotten.

Fading away

When Jo saw her dad again, she was shocked. She knew he was sick—even though he didn't mention it, it was easy to see. His eyes were cloudy, tinged with yellow, with dark circles around them. His skin had a different hue to it, and his stomach was hard and swollen. Dad pretended there was nothing wrong.

Jo told Gramma GreyGrouse how he looked; soon the old woman came out to visit him personally. She brought dandelion root and left it, with no word of explanation beyond "it's good for your guts." Jo's dad started eating it regularly. The list of things that his stomach would tolerate was shrinking, and sure enough the root was something he could digest. His drinking went down to zero: his body simply couldn't take any more poison.

Jo drove up to see her dad often that year. If the car wasn't working she'd take the Greyhound, and sometimes Newt drove her. Her dad didn't like Newt when he first met him. He said to her privately, "Oh, Jo—what's up now? What are you doing? He's too old for you." Jo never repeated what he'd said to Newt, and after a few more visits her dad conceded that Newt was "okay."

Each visit her father's body seemed to shrink, his bulk shrivelling up inside his frame as the cancer ate him up, for that's what he had, cancer of the liver. Finally, he'd been to the doctor and was diagnosed. Not that it changed anything, there was nothing they could do. The doctor told him he had advanced liver cancer and that he'd probably not make it much longer than three months.

Though his body was fading away, he seemed to Jo to be more expansive each time she came to visit. Always, through the drinking and the sober periods, his basic nature was pleasant and cheerful. Even sick, he was always joking around, always trying to make everyone else feel happy. He took his illness in stride; a defiance towards the verdict of the doctor surfaced and it seemed he kept going on nothing but willpower for more than a year.

At the end of his life, all he ate was raw hamburger and dandelion root. They were the only things left that he could keep down, and finally they weren't enough.

There were only a few people at the funeral. The man who was the recipient of her hatred—the only hatred Jo had ever allowed hersef—had the nerve to ask if he could be a pallbearer. Jo was strong enough to tell him that if he showed up at the funeral—or if she ever saw his face again—there would be two funerals. Jo and Sam clung together at the graveside, more alone than they'd ever been in their lives, and neither one could think of a single thing to say.

Newt was fun to live with; he was the sword for her scabbard, and Jo was happy. They never talked about getting married, and that was fine with Jo. They were both readers, and it was nice to sit in quiet companionship in the living room in the winter, the warmth of the wood fire cocooning them. Newt always had opinions on everything, and he was interesting to talk to. During the summers Newt liked to travel around. Jo liked it too; she liked jumping in the Cadillac and rolling down the highway.

One of Newt's favourite places to go was the Kootenays, a mountainous region in southeastern BC. The skinny highway with all its corners and mountains, the ferry ride, it was all fun for Jo. She'd phoned and cancelled her shifts so many times that she'd had to quit work; they didn't want to give her any more time off. Her resolution to stay away from men was tucked firmly on the other side of Newt; she felt as though she'd landed in a safe place. Newt was a gentleman who lived up to the word. He always said, "I'm a lover, not a fighter."

One day they found themselves at a dinner party at the home of a friend of a friend in the Kootenays. One of the guests cornered Newt and kept showing off a chunk of gold that he said he prospected out of his claim. He kept including Jo in the conversation, even though she'd consistently not held his gaze; he seemed like such a braggart to her. The nugget he kept showing around was shiny from coming in and out of his pocket; didn't he know real gold miners never showed their pouch in public?

Apparently Newt didn't know, because the next day they were headed to Grand Forks, just to "check it out." It didn't look like much to Jo when they walked over the claim, but Newt saw more potential than she did. They went to town and got a claims map and spent a few weeks rambling around with two pans, trying to get colour in every little sand bar on every little creek they found. Jo learned about getting colour, and every once in a while they'd get a few grains of gold in their pans. Then Newt would pore over the maps and shake his head—"nope, that's pretty well all taken"—and off to the next creek they'd go. For Jo, it was an exciting time, roaming around trying to find gold, sometimes in such beautiful places. They had a tent and a thin ground mattress, a camp stove and cooler, and many a time she could fish their supper from a mountain stream while Newt checked for gold in the sediment.

Jo got excited about the gold, but Newt got the fever. He couldn't quit thinking about the claim of the man with the big nugget. Jo tried to explain how she felt about that man and his claim, but Newt couldn't hear her. Whenever they were in a town they'd get a room where they could shower, and Jo would hunt down the local laundromat and get their clothes washed and dried. Newt would treat them to dinner, and usually they'd end up in the hotel bar where Newt would talk gold to anyone who would listen. The more he learned, the more he was certain that the first claim they'd seen was the best one.

"You see, Jo, most of the creek bottoms have been scouted out by now, and all the good places have been staked. So the best bet is to buy one of the claims that hasn't been worked much. And that place is the perfect spot. You can see that the creek used to flow higher up the walls of that hill. Any gold that was washed downstream in earlier times is going to be imbedded in the till on that hillside. That's a big nugget he had, and I don't even care if it's the biggest one—a handful half that size would be pretty nice."

"Newt, what if he didn't even get it from there? What if he won it in a poker game or something like that?"

"Why would a guy do that? It's not like it's driving up the cost of the claim. What he's asking is a reasonable price; it's the going rate for an unworked piece of ground. Everyone says every claim has the price of itself in gold somewhere waiting to be found, and I'll bet this one has a hell of a lot more than that."

Eventually Newt headed the car into Vancouver to see his mother, dropping Jo off at a friend's place to visit. He spent the night with his mother and picked Jo up on the way out of town the next day. He was in a really good mood, and when they stopped in Chilliwack for supper, Newt ordered a bottle of wine and paid for it with a wallet that was much fuller than it had been the day before. He grinned at her when he saw she noticed. "And that's not all!" He pulled a thin note from between the bills and showed Jo the biggest cheque she'd ever seen. Her eyes widened; she looked for explanations.

Newt grinned. "For the claim. The old lady put up the capital for the claim and a grand for operating expenses till we get some gold." He waved the wallet. "And a little cash infusion as well. Thank you, Momma."

And with that, Newt became the sole owner of a bend in the creek by Grand Forks, including the "works."

Are we idle?

One day in 2012, Jo and I are on the phone, and she wonders if I've heard about Idle No More. I haven't.

She says, "It's a protest movement. It's new. It's about taking a stand for what's right. It's mostly Native people, but it's right across society, not just Natives. I'd say more environmentalists: they're saying to wake up and do something about what's happening to the world."

"What are they doing?"

"They're holding protests and rallies. All peaceful. You should look them up on the computer." I agree to do that later on in the day. We're in a funny position, Jo and I; we're like a news team. I don't listen to TV or radio much, but I spend a lot of time on the computer. Computers may be the best thing about this lifetime (right up there next to hot baths). It's so amazing that now any person with a smart phone has access to the accumulated knowledge of mankind, and they can hold it in their one hand. Jo doesn't do computers, but she listens to the radio and to TV. Often, she tells me what to research and then I report back to her what the computer heaves up.

What it heaves up this time is interesting. #IdleNoMore is the hashtag and logo of four women from Saskatchewan. They are young, educated women, and they say it is time for the voices for the earth to speak up and be heard. Their message is both imperative and timely. They are using social media to spread their message, and they have birthed a movement. The message to speak up and be heard has resonated worldwide, and there are people all over the globe using the logo.

Idle No More is calling for action; they say that a silent voice implies agreement, that it is time to reconsider other values besides money, and that the earth can wait no longer.

At this time, there is a big focus on Chief Theresa Spence; she's camped out on an island in the Ottawa River near Parliament Hill, on a hunger strike to try to force the government to recognize the plight of her people in Attawapiskat. There they are, a traditionally nomadic people, moved into a remote reserve in northern Ontario that is poor, very poor. Their town water comes from a slough and is not good to drink. Almost half the band lives off-reserve, and yet the housing can't keep up with the population growth. The reserve was built in the sixties, so the houses are getting pretty worn out. There are a few new ones, but not nearly enough. There is a strong connection between Chief Theresa and Idle No More.

The media is having a heyday with the Chief. They say she isn't really on a hunger strike; she's on a restricted liquid diet, which isn't quite the same thing.

Fish broth, medicinal tea, and lemon water may be enough to live on, although not enough to have much of an energy reserve.

She's complaining about Bill C-45, saying that it will take protection away from the land, and that it is another move by the federal government to disenfranchise Native claims. She's getting a huge amount of publicity, and although the facts point to the appropriateness of her stand, lots of the reports are negative. The government is poking too: they are releasing information that makes it seem as though she's a crook who is making herself and her common-law husband rich while her people go cold and hungry. The media plays this up to the hilt. This is made very clear later on, when I'm on Facebook talking to relatives in Ontario.

"She's nothing but a fake and a crook," they write.

It started out by them saying they were surprised I wasn't out with Idle No More, and me replying that I'd just heard about it and was going to join lickety-split.

They must have been joking because it set off a rant. "The chiefs are taking millions for themselves; she pays herself more than the Prime Minister of Canada; she pays her boyfriend $850 a day for not keeping the books; she runs the reserve like a communist dictatorship and the diamond mine and the government have poured hundreds of millions of dollars into that reserve that have simply disappeared."

Another couple hours of Googling and reading discloses the half-truths. The upturned bucket of money from the mine flowed into a trust fund and the real figure seems to be $10.3 million in the fund plus another $2 million annually in royalties. The hundreds of millions from the government are really $90 million, and that is over lots of years, so the annual figure is much lower. The messages our relatives are receiving vastly distort the truth.

The Idle No More movement has gained a figurehead in Chief Theresa Spence, whether the original founders in Saskatchewan wanted her or not. Those women have also made a list of contentious issues. One of them is the Doctrine of Discovery. Another is the pipelines that are planned to drain the oil sands and the shale gas of the western prairies out through the mountains of BC. They want recognition of inherent land title, and recognition of equality in governance with Canada. They want treaties to be honoured in the spirit they were made.

They believe that the best hope for environmental protection is to use the wisdom of the Native people when considering resource development. They have some strong associates—Wab Kinew shows up again. Jo will like to hear that.

Chimney fire

Fall in the north is incredibly beautiful. The second growth of alfalfa is still green in the field, and the trees have all turned to orange and red, the contrast making it look as though we're living in a postcard. This magnificent time of the year is the signal for Northerners to flee to Arizona or else hunker down for the winter: gather the firewood, clean out the gardens, and tidy up the yards. Early in the fall, Jo lights her fire in the mornings, then lets it die out. It takes the chill out of the crisp mornings.

Later on in November, when the colourful display of September has faded to humble browns and greys, Jo keeps the fire lit full-time, getting up in the really cold nights to add to it. This particular morning, Jo puts a good load in the stove and leaves it wide open. There's no snow on the ground yet and there are still things she can do in the yard. Today, she's putting compost on top of where she put the garlic and side dressing the fruit trees. On the phone the next day, she tells about it. "I was out in the front yard, and you know Jake and Annie's son? No? Well he's about mid-twenties, and I'm standing out in the yard talking to him, and his eyes get real big looking past me, and he says, "Fire!" and I turn around, and by God there is fire, and it's up in the new roof. You can see the chimney's red hot, and sparks are coming out all around it, and they're sparking right onto the boards from under the roof, and they're catching them on fire. Thankfully, there was a hose hooked up and it wasn't frozen, and I ran around the side and got it, and he climbed up there lickety-split and hosed it out. I ran in the house and poured water directly in the stove, till it ran out. We put it out."

"Are you ever lucky!"

"Yeah! That's for sure. And he and his dad are so nice. He came over right away, too, and between the two of them they pulled out that part of the chimney, went to town and got a length of insulated pipe, and put it down through both roofs, right to the inside. Now it can't catch on fire like that again. Those two were mad because the guy didn't put insulated pipe through it when he built it, but it's not really his fault. I told him I didn't want him to do anything that went too far above the money I had. I don't have the money now but the hardware store let me have an account there, so I put a down payment on the pipe and I can finish paying for it next month.

"Oh—and good news, this week another guy is coming to take off the tin and put a vapour barrier under it. Then, with any luck, it shouldn't leak anymore."

Newt and Jo settled into a routine when his mother bought the gold mine. They spent the summers down in the Kootenays and the winters in Endako. When the first signs of spring appeared up north, Newt would start getting impatient, and Jo would start packing all the stuff she'd want to have with her in the summer, and it wouldn't be long till they headed south. Spring arrives in Grand Forks much sooner than it does in Endako.

It was exciting getting things ready to go. Newt was a good mechanic, and he could see ways to set up the equipment so the claim could be worked easily. It wasn't like hard rock mining where the gold has flowed underground in a vein; this was "placer gold." Tiny flecks of it were mixed with the glacial till and needed to be separated by water and gravity. Gold is the heaviest and will sink to the bottom of the pan when the soil is agitated with water. Jo learned how to pan quickly and efficiently. Often, when a shovel full of muck was washing out on the screen, Newt and Jo were shaking part of it out in their pans. There was always a little, never a lot—just enough to draw them on. Every once in a while they'd find a decent-sized nugget but never one as big as the previous owner had displayed. Jo was sure he'd lied to them. The claim had hardly been touched when they arrived on the scene, and it was unlikely he'd found the nugget lying exposed in the creek bed, seeing as how close it was to Grand Forks and how many times the creeks had all been panned over the last hundred years. She kept silent about her suspicions and didn't say anything to dampen Newt's excitement. He was in a gold fever, thinking about nothing else. He'd get up in the morning, eat a hasty breakfast, and then get outside and get busy. It seemed to Jo like they worked non-stop for weeks, not getting sidetracked by anything, running full tilt on hope. They were collecting gold a few grains at a time, but it was starting to add up. Newt always bought the paper when he went to town; he was waiting for gold to go up so he could sell. They were getting pretty broke again because Newt had champagne tastes on a beer budget. So far, his mother kept them going and often she'd send a cheque in the mail.

Newt never seemed to feel bad about this. He assured Jo the "old lady" loved him, and she had lots of money. Besides, they'd pay her back when they got a decent stake from the claim.

Both of them worked hard; there was nothing easy about mining. Everything was hard and heavy, and many nights they fell exhausted into the bed in the trailer till dawn called them out again the next day. Both grew lean and muscled, brown from the mountain sun, he with his bronze tan and she with her long, dark hair tumbling past her shoulders, deep brown tan from head to toe, and not a spare ounce of fat on either one. They thrived on the work; it was the happiest period of both their lives—young, healthy, in love, content.

They learned to stretch the food money, something Jo already knew about. She'd buy the cheaper things like beans and rice, things that went a long way when the cans and the junk food were finished. One day, Newt went in to buy groceries with the last of their money and didn't come back to the claim for three days. Jo ate beans, boiled navy beans with the last of the ketchup and mustard cooked in for flavouring. She wondered where he'd got to but wasn't too worried, mostly she was lonely. The big bucket had broken down; she thought Newt had most likely taken it into his head to go get the part they needed. She went out picking the huckleberries that grew very well all around the claim. There were gophers that weren't scared of people, and Jo was fascinated by them. She took a few cooked beans with her every time she went out, and soon they would take them right from her fingertips. It was the most alone Jo had ever been. With no one else for miles, she longed for company. Just before Newt arrived back she was sitting by the creek, letting it talk to her and soothe her need for companionship when she noticed a dog out of the corner of her eye. It was sitting about fifteen feet away from her, head cocked to one side like he was wondering what she was doing.

Jo moved slowly and held out her hand, making a quiet kissing noise. "Come here, boy." To her pleasure, the dog immediately came over and sat closer, almost within reach. Jo reached in her pocket for the bag with the remaining two cooked beans and offered them to the dog. He reached out his nose and sniffed them but didn't take them. Jo put them on the ground in between them and moved back. The dog stood up, ate the beans, and then sat down again. Jo patted her leg and the dog came closer, letting her briefly stroke his shoulder before stepping back out of range. The dog followed her around all afternoon, staying just out of reach, keeping her company and wagging his tail when Jo spoke to him. She had just decided to keep him and care for him when he came close, nuzzled her hand, turned, and trotted away. Jo looked after the disappearing dog with an abrupt sense of personal loss, puzzled about the hasty departure. Within a few moments she heard the sound of a car motor. Ah, Newt had returned.

He was in a great mood. The car was full of groceries and he'd bought them new gloves, a new sun hat for her, and some needles for beading that she'd wanted, as well as the part they needed. He was refreshed and raring to go. Later, he told her he'd looked at the pathetic amount of money had left and decided right then and there to phone his mother and ask for an advance. He had waited in town till the cheque arrived. The hotel had let him keep a tab till then. Jo had a moment of envy—he'd been in town at the hotel living it up while she'd been at the claim, lonely, with her gold pan shaking out bits of gold for him. It didn't seem quite fair, but she bottled that thought up and set to making the best meal she'd had for weeks.

Jo is on the phone. "Well the tin has been removed, the membrane installed underneath, and the tin screwed back on. Hallelujah!"

"Finally," I say. "Finally. I hope this time it is fixed for good, not simply till it thaws out!"

"Only time will tell," she says and I hear confidence in her tone. This is a good thing, a long time coming. The original carpenter didn't want to fix it. He said it wasn't the problem, that there was a free flow of air through the roof that forestalled frost buildup under the tin. Jo got a different handyman to come do the job after that verdict, but she can't hide her contempt for the bad work ethic. "He didn't come and try to figure out why the damn thing leaks, just told me it couldn't," she fumes. "At least this guy just did it. I can't take much more of this roof leaking. I feel like I've gone to great effort to deal with this problem and it simply won't go away."

"Not for want of trying," I agree. She's been fixing this problem for years already. I can hardly believe it was still leaking, as though it was defying being waterproof.

It gets real warm in December. That's been happening more and more as the climate changes. There are three days in a row that are plus ten, and I phone Jo to brag a bit. She's not even pretending to laugh at my attempt at my humour. I finally ask what's wrong, and I'm not even surprised at the answer.

"I give up. I simply give up. I'll put the pots in the right spots, and I'll rearrange the furniture so plants can live directly under the leaks. I'm not going to worry about it anymore. I'm done fixing the roof. I'm going to learn to live with it."

I understand her frustration. Roofing is not rocket science; it should be easy to fix a leaky roof. I am a methodical person, and I figure there has to be a reason for a leaky roof that rain and snow cannot penetrate, nor condensation build up underneath. The answer has to be closer down. The trailer roof must be building it up on the bottom side of the roofing, above the ceiling line where she can't see it. By now the fires should have dried out everything. The humidity levels must be close to zero inside, and I think it must be the vents from the plumbing that are the culprits. I suggest this.

"I don't fucking care. I tell you I simply am not going to give this any more space. I'm not going to think about it, I'm not going to talk about it. When it leaks I'll put a pot under it, and when it doesn't I'll not think about it. Never talk about this again to me. Tell me instead about your new grandbaby. Did you get to see her on the weekend?"

I don't talk about it anymore to her but I make an internal vow: if I ever win the lottery or get lots of money I'm going to make sure her roof gets fixed. And I don't even need to ask because I'm not allowed to talk about it.

... Newt gets bored

For five years, Newt and Jo kept the mining pace up. In the fall each year they'd have enough gold to live for the winter, but they never had enough to pay back his loans or buy the loader that would make their job that much easier. Newt bragged to other people and made it sound like they were getting rich. He didn't tell anyone else that he was working the claim on his parents' money and neither did Jo.

She knew it was starting to wear on him a bit because he started drinking on a regular basis. Jo noticed when he brought a bottle home with him on one of his town trips. She'd noticed the town trips were more frequent; she was used to him getting antsy and leaving soon after running out of tobacco, and now it seemed he'd do the same thing with booze. As soon as the bottle was empty he'd be finding a reason to go to town, never saying it was for the booze, but always returning with another bottle. When Jo mentioned it he told her he didn't need someone to count his drinks, that he was a grown man and he could take care of that himself. Jo vowed not to nag him, even when she saw it was getting out of hand.

One day, she'd gone to town with him. They'd broken another piece that had brought them to a standstill, and Newt knew he'd have to order the part on the phone from Vancouver and wait for the bus to deliver it before there was any more work done. The part came unexpectedly quickly—up on the evening bus—and Newt had been socializing in the pub for most the day when Jo came to the bar with the good news and told him everything else was done, laundry and all. "I guess there's no need to stay another night; it'll just cost extra for nothing," he conceded and they headed back to the claim. Newt had seemed okay in town, but as soon as they were out on the highway he seemed pretty drunk, unable to drive in a straight line. He kept swerving over the centre line.

"Let me drive," she suggested.

"Let you drive this beautiful car? Do I look crazy?" he asked.

"No, you look drunk."

"I'm not too drunk to drive this goddamn car. I'd have to be a lot drunker than this before I'd bloody well let you drive my good car," he fumed.

Jo was silent, but not because she agreed with him; she watched the road closely, ready to yell if he did something worse than swerving. It was a good thing she was watching, because he got sleepy as well as sloppy, and when she saw the bridge marker coming in the lights she let out a shriek that woke him up and refocused him on his driving.

"Oops, didn't see that bugger coming at me," he observed. Jo didn't answer. She was so pissed, she vowed she wouldn't go to town with him again.

Jo kept her promise to herself, and the next times Newt went to town she stayed at the claim. The dog showed up shortly after Newt left each time and kept her company. If it wasn't for the footprints that she showed him he might think she was making up the dog. There were more people in the neighbourhood. A young couple lived a few miles upstream, and Newt had brought them over one time on his way home from town. Jo hadn't been expecting anyone; she was busy cleaning out the sluice box. It was an all-day job, one that she'd been putting off for weeks. It really was a two-person job, but Newt hadn't shown too much enthusiasm for doing it the last few times he was back, and Jo didn't want to put it off any longer.

Her arms ached from panning. On a visit to her father before he'd passed away he'd given her a fibreglass pan that was much lighter than the steel one she'd used before. She was grateful for the lightweight pan that day; a person had to pan every bit of the sluice before it was returned to the stream. If the riffles on the steel hadn't caught the gold, nor the long hunk of carpet where the finer particles were supposed to catch, the last chance to get it was the sluice box where the fines settled after the last wash. That meant the fines were really small, but if a person was patient each time the painstaking process was complete then there would be a little flash in the pan. When Jo heard the car coming, she first shrugged back into the clothes she'd abandoned in the heat of the afternoon, and then swept the dust into her poke and tucked it into her shorts pocket.

A nice pickup followed Newt in, containing a man and a woman: Shane, tall, dark, and bearded, and Barbara, blond and looking like she'd stepped out of the Simpsons-Sears catalogue. Jo nodded as Newt made the introductions, self-conscious of the dirt she was covered in, legs and arms covered in the fine silt that only the sluice box contains, clean hands and wrists making a marked contrast. The woman, Barbara, acknowledged the introduction with a nod as well, a distant nod, and Jo felt repulsed by the woman instantly. She wasn't sure if the woman's disdain was because Jo was "Indian" or because she was dirty. She felt the woman's eyes rake her up and down and dismiss her. Jo was instantly angry, and the fact that Newt was more than a little drunk didn't help. She knew Newt well enough by now that there was no mistaking the flirting he was doing with the blond bimbo. And right in front of her husband, too. Jo looked closer at the husband, wondering what he made of it but the husband laughed each time Newt made an inappropriate comment and thought it was the best of fun. Jo didn't know what to make of it herself; none of them seemed to care if she was there or not, so she walked away. No one called out to her. She walked downstream and around the corner to the hole where she usually bathed and sunk herself in the creek, going right under and letting the water wash the dirt out of her hair, wishing she could wash her feelings as easily. As she'd cleaned the sluice box she'd imagined Newt coming back, seeing what she'd done in his absence, and being grateful. Instead he came home and treated her to a shot of rejection. Tears of self-pity welled in her eyes and she stayed away till the people left. Newt was already on the bed snoring when she got to the trailer, and she wondered if they'd waited till he passed out to leave or if he'd lasted till they said their good-byes. Jo made the table down into a bed and that's where she went to sleep.

In the morning she rose before Newt and was already panning out the sluice again when he wandered down, pan in hand. "Holy God, Jo, you're almost done. You must have been working on this for days."

At least he noticed! "No, just yesterday. If you help, we should be done by noon." The poke that she'd contemplated dumping, in her upset from the day before, weighed heavy in her pocket. She pulled it out and tossed it to him. He grinned, hefted it, opened it, and stirred the contents with his finger. "Must be better than two ounces. Did you weigh it?"

"No. You got back before I was finished." The memory brought back the bitterness, and Jo looked away. If Newt had any concept of how she felt he didn't show it. He helped pan, taking his shirt off as soon as the summer sun hit the valley. He sweated far more than the work called for and it smelled sour, fouling the air around him. Jo sadly recognized the smell of alcohol departing his body through its pores; she noticed his belly was white again and he was start-ing to pack a little fat around his middle, something she hadn't seen since the year she met him. Then she tried to recall the last time he'd helped pan and realized it had been a very long time. He chatted about the couple he'd brought home, talked about the equipment they were using, said he'd like to go see their claim. He didn't notice Jo's silence, and he kept talking at her, not to her. After a couple hours he said he was going to take a quick dip because he smelled, and Jo was happy he'd at least noticed he stunk. She came in to make lunch and Newt came in smelling and looking much better. He was packing a pail of water and Jo was again surprised. When was the last time he'd packed the water? He poured a kettle full and after it was heated enough he shaved, face leaning into the little round mirror on the end of the cupboard, patting aftershave on his cheeks when he was finished.

He'd brought home fresh peaches and yogurt, one of Jo's favourite snacks. She cut the peaches into the yogurt for dessert and ate with satisfaction. She thought about peaches as being a little bit of heaven on earth. She'd like to plant a peach tree. Wouldn't it be nice to pick peaches right in your own yard, she thought to herself. Newt wasn't hungry, just thirsty. He got dressed in clothes way too nice to pan sluice with. "The rest can wait for another day," he told Jo. "Let's go over to Barbara and Shane's and have a look at what they're doing."

"It'll only take a few more hours and the sluice will be empty. We should finish that first. There will still be lots of daylight after that."

"This car and me are going visiting. Come on now, we'll finish that tomorrow."

"Come on, Newt, tomorrow is when you're going to get that bucket going again. You been saying that for a couple weeks already." Jo let her frustration show in her voice.

"I'm telling you it doesn't matter whether the sluice gets done today, whether the bucket gets fixed tomorrow. It doesn't matter."

"Why not, Newt? Why doesn't it matter? Why am I busting my ass here if it doesn't matter?"

"In the long run, none of it matters."

"Does it matter that you owe your mom so much? How are you ever going to make it pay here if you don't work?"

"What the hell are you talking about? I don't work? What the hell do you think I've been doing here? Playing?"

"I'm not saying you never worked here, I'm saying you haven't lately."

"If a person forgets to have fun, to have friends, it isn't worth it."

Jo stayed silent. He was going to town by himself all the time, and sometimes he'd stay for a couple days. Occasionally, he'd be home the same night. Wasn't she a friend anymore? Didn't he think she needed a friend too? She sure wasn't going to visit Barbara; she'd made it plain in one look that they'd never be friends. Newt could go there but she wasn't going to.

"Come on," he said. "The time off will do you good."

Jo shook her head, and he shrugged, turned on his heel and left, spinning the tires in the car as he departed. Jo went back to the job, realizing as she did that Newt still had the poke. She had a spare and started filling it with the few grains she'd glean each time from the bottom of her pan. There was a rhythm to the job; after a short while the shoulder and arm muscles would lose their morning ache and get into the groove. She'd fill a bucket with the fines, carry it down to the river, and pan it out patiently, pan after pan, washed for the last time and released back into the river that once deposited it eons ago. It made Jo feel like she was part of a circle, and the work passed pleasantly enough. One pan sifted out a fair sized nugget, and Jo was amazed. It should never have made it past the screen, let alone through the carpet. It was a satisfying addition to the poke. Twilight reddened the sky when Jo finished, another couple ounces to the good. Newt hadn't made it back from his visit by morning, so Jo spent the next day putting everything back together and went to bed satisfied with her day's work. As soon as Newt got the bucket fixed they'd be rolling again.

The Seven Sacred Fires

Jo comes to visit a few days early. We're going on a road trip and will be gone about three weeks, and she's going to watch the farm for us. She listens to CBC a lot and tells me things I haven't heard. She's saved items of interest in her head that she wants to know more about and gets me to Google them. This time she wants me to look up the Seven Sacred Fire prophecies. It's Wab Kinew again. She says I should pay attention to Wab Kinew; he is very wise for a young guy. I look up the prophecies and the hair prickles on the back of my neck when I read them.

These are prophecies that predate the European "discovery" of America, and they are the reason that some indigenous people moved inland from the east coast before Contact. I read them out loud from Wikipedia and we discuss them. Jo says, "'The place the food grows on water,' that's wild rice and it's Manitoba."

"Maybe we had a shot at changing things then, the stand of the Métis," I say.

"Yeah, well, we know how that ended! Maybe if the leader wasn't so crazy holy, it would have had a chance."

"I agree, those priests had him twisted up in circles. Give me his buddy to follow, Gabriel Dumont."

Now that we've resettled the Métis situation, we go on reading about the Sacred Fires. It's chilling. They clearly foretold the past few centuries: the coming of the "light skinned race," the advice to beware of the reality that has coalesced around us. "…the rivers run with poison and fish become unfit to eat" stops us dead. The words close

144 — Not My Fate

my throat up—that's happening! I look at Jo and there are tears in her eyes. That's how I feel too, and so we sit up at the office in front of the computer and we cry for what's gone wrong. It's a while before can read the rest. We have to tease each other out of it. I say, sniffing back my runny nose and wiping my tears on my sleeve, "Two menopausal women fixing the affairs of the world!"

"Damn right!" she wipes up her own watery eyes, gives a weak grin, and goes and gets us both a tissue to blow into.

"Ready now?" I go and she nods. We run with the words, we shout "smallpox and TB" and Jo adds "diabetes."

When we get to the fifth and the false promises, Jo says, "treaties" and I say "Jesus." We look at each other and say, "you're right" at the same time. Then we nod: it could be both.

The sixth clearly means residential schools to both of us. And the new sickness in the schools was not just the deadly new diseases, it was also spiritual sickness, trading the rich heritage of the people and their relationship with the earth for the promise of an afterlife that seemed much poorer than the afterlife promised by their traditions, and where they could at best be still inferior on account of their skin colour.

Jo wonders out loud, "I wonder what a mine manager would say if you told him the earth was alive and quite feminine, that she had distributed the resources in a way that was as important to her as the arrangement of his nervous network inside his body was to him."

"He'd yell 'Security! Call First Aid! There's a delusional woman in here!'"

We laugh, but both of us know it's true. We've talked about it before. There's so much no one understands. We know electromagnetics so little, and we have no true understanding of time. If there were a picture showing what we know and what we don't know, then what we don't know would take up most the space. And by science's own definitions we are walking containers of mostly space, held together by some undefined co-operative force. There's so much we don't know that we should be erring on the side of caution. What if everyone treated the earth as if she were alive, as if she were our mother? What if oil is where it is on purpose, and what if it's performing a function that we're not aware of? What if the gold in the ground is conducting electromagnetic waves from the sun? There are too many what ifs.

The seventh prophecy leaves us some room for hope. Both of us think that is where we are now on the timeline of the prophecies. There is a choice between two roads: we can choose a higher path than the one that pounds us towards the precipice of environmental collapse. We can turn away from that and instill different values. That's the promise of the seventh; the threat is that if we don't choose this other path, this bend in the trail, we will "cause much suffering and death to all Earth's people."

"I choose," Jo says, "I choose to change."

"Oh, if someone could just invent a benign way for us to power up! That would make things so much easier; we're all so used to having power at our fingertips. Tractors and Rototillers, and trucks to bring us compost. We're so spoiled with the hot baths on demand, the freezers to store food, and the chainsaws to cut up the firewood. Maybe we've come too far to turn away now," I worry.

"We don't have to do it all ourselves;we simply have to embrace the changes. Those New People, don't you think Wab Kinew is one?"

I saw him on an interview with George Stroumboulopoulos and she could be right. He seemed very smart. "Most likely."

"We don't have to do everything ourselves, but we do have to be ready for the changes, and for these new young people. We have to be ready to be the crones, the elders. These young people, they're the ones who are going to make it right," Jo says, and I hope she's right.

Meeting the earth people

Newt's heart went out of gold mining. What had been the one and only spurt of pure ambition in Newt's whole life hit the ground and fizzled out. He'd come back and got the bucket running, they'd put through about twenty-five yards of material, and then the pump motor broke down again. In a previous year, Newt would have made some funny comment, figured out what was wrong with it, and gone to town and got whatever it needed to make it work again. Even if he drank, he still got things done. The Newt this year wasn't inclined to be funny. When the pump broke down he sank down on the bench they'd made beside the works, head in his hands, a picture of abject misery. Jo sat down beside him. "It's just a pump. Not the end of the world."

"It's not the pump. It's this whole scene: work, work, work and nothing much to show for it. If I was up north and got the Cat running, then at least I'd make some decent money and wouldn't have to work like a slave to do it."

Jo thought to herself that it was the first time in weeks that Newt had worked for more than two days without finding some excuse for going to town, and this was the first time he'd work, work, worked for several months. She didn't have much sympathy for him, but she was carrying the social habit of trying to make everyone feel good, and that everyone included Newt.

"Look how much we got done in only four days."

He shook his head, stood up slowly, shoulders rounded down and walked to the trailer. He poured himself a whiskey and chugged it down straight. After a couple ounces he was in a better mood and gave Jo a hug when he came back outside, a thing which would have been nicer without the whiskey breath, but she understood what he was doing; she'd seen plenty of people coping with things by using alcohol as their ally. Newt left in the morning. He packed a suitcase and told Jo if they didn't have the part in Kamloops then he might drive to Vancouver and pick it up himself, and maybe see the old lady while he was down there. She knew that meant he'd be gone for three, maybe four days. There wasn't much to do while he was gone. Without the pump the works didn't work, and that was a good thing because her wrists were so sore she thought the rest would do them good. They had a good store of food in, and Jo had a box of books she hadn't read, so she said "goodbye" and "have a good trip" with sincerity, glad of the chance to be alone with nothing to do.

The berries were ripe, there were herbs she wanted to gather, and she knew where some of them grew. The dog seemed to have a sixth sense for when she was alone; he came with her on long forages through the woods. Sometimes he'd reach out with his muzzle to sniff her, but he didn't much like to be touched. He wouldn't take food from her hand; he'd eat it as soon as it was placed on the ground, as though it was fair game only after it left her hand. Jo called him Dog, and talked to him like he was a person. Sometimes he seemed to understand, but a lot of the time he just seemed puzzled by her, sitting on his haunches and watching with his head cocked to one side, one ear up, one ear down.

The first few days were filled with a peace that Jo luxuriated in. There was no one in the whole world she had to answer to, no need to prove herself to anyone because no one was there. It was a profound experience, and one that she'd missed while she was so busy worrying and trying to do the work for the both of them. She slid into a routine with her days: she'd get up and make coffee, read while it brewed, and then while she drank it. After that, she'd heat a kettle full of water, then wash up, braid her hair, and head outside. She always put on a hat because she hated having the sun glare off her glasses. Newt used to joke to her that the only thing she should ever wear was the hat, nothing else. He said that when he closed his eyes, that was how he'd picture her. It always made her laugh when he said it, partly from embarrassment, partly from pleasure. She knew she looked good, with no fat but plenty of curves, lean and muscled from the hard work, and glowing deep brown from the sun, head to toe.

Once outside, she would pack the water for the trailer and gather up twigs and deadwood for the outdoor fire that she lit on cool evenings, and sometimes even on warm ones if the bugs were too bad. Most of the day she spent picking berries or collecting herbs, timing her forages for after the dew burned off and before the absolute heat of the day. In the afternoons when it got too hot she'd swim in the creek and dry off in the sun, read for a while, get hot, go back in, and repeat the process.

Jo had never cared about reading a book from cover to cover; she sometimes had a dozen on the go. She had picked up a book on birds from the second-hand store and found it invaluable more than once. Birds became a lot friendlier when the noise of the works wasn't disturbing the peace. They would come close by, hopping sideways and watching her while they sidled in to pick up a morsel that she'd strategically placed close by. She figured out which bird was making each call and soon could tell exactly who was talking. After about ten days, she was beginning to feel like she was the only person left on the face of the earth. She thought to herself, "I wonder if something happened to me how long it would be before someone knew I was missing?" and it felt to her that she was very alone. Who cared?

After two weeks, Newt still hadn't come back. Jo was running out of food. She'd already used all her menstrual pads and had stuffed moss in cheesecloth for the last couple days. The propane ran out in the trailer, but that should have been no big deal because they had an extra tank and she could change it. She hadn't done it before; it was something she'd entrusted to Newt because she wasn't that comfortable around gas. For this same reason she used the kerosene lamp, putting up with the feeble lighting rather than pumping up and lighting the hissing monster of the naphtha-fired lantern. Newt kept saying he was going to hook up propane lights in the trailer, but Jo was happy that that chore was one of those that he kept postponing.

When she went to change the propane tank, she couldn't loosen the nut. She put a bar on it and still the nut didn't budge. Then she wondered if she was turning it the wrong way, reversed directions, and off it came. The tank was light as a feather and she lifted it away easily. She grabbed the other one and, to her dismay, realized it was also light as a feather. Empty. Damn Newt, he was supposed to have filled it weeks ago. She hoped he'd be home soon: she was out of almost everything and now she'd have to cook on the outside fire.

She'd been quilting and beading in her spare hours, and now she spent increasing time doing both. She ran out of sewing thread first, and then a few days later ran out of beading thread. She was glad for both the rice and the beans; it was a lot better than the alternative, a straight wild berry diet. She found both wild onion and mint to use for flavouring.

Jo was getting more anxious as the days passed. She wondered if something had happened to Newt, and what if no one in the world knew where she was? Another part of herself argued that his mother knew she was up here, and if anything had happened, she would send word to Jo. She didn't know how long Newt had been gone. At first she didn't keep good track of time, but as near as she could figure it had been about three weeks already. Jo made up her mind that if he wasn't back soon she'd pack up and leave. She would only have to walk a few miles before she would be on a big enough road to have traffic and then she could hitchhike. She'd read all the books already and was rereading them by the dim light of the kerosene lamp. She stayed up very late each night and got up early—the hours in between didn't seem to be sleeping ones, mostly half-awake dreams. She spent more hours in the woods, coaxing the gophers to accept beans and talking to the birds, trying to make the sounds in their language. She had always liked animals, but now it seemed like they returned her good regard. The fox that trotted through camp every morning checking to see if she'd left anything out for him stopped and gazed back at her for a minute, panting through his mouth once in a gesture that looked oddly like a smile before he trotted off. He seemed almost human; Jo wanted to tell him to stay but lacked the diction. She was hungry for meat. She eyed up the rabbit Dog dragged in, and though she doubted she'd have stooped so low as to steal from the dog, he seemed to sense her thoughts and disappeared back into the bush with his catch. It struck Jo's funny bone and she laughed and laughed.

That evening while lying on the bed reading she began to smell something in the trailer. She got up and smelled her herbs, wondering if she'd gathered some strong smelling plant by accident. Smelling everything didn't solve the mystery. She shrugged, lay back down, and resumed reading but the smell came back to her, magnified. She closed her eyes, concentrated only on smell. Where was it coming from? The smell increased in intensity and now it was accompanied by a noise, a whisper like slippers on the floor. She opened her eyes and squinted into the shadow cast by her body from the coal oil lamp. There were little people in the trailer, standing right in front of her! Not children—little people, and maybe not people. The closest one looked old: he had a cane. He looked jolly, like he was ready to break into laughter and his mood was contagious. Jo did laugh out loud, a quizzical, half-believing laugh. She wondered to herself if they were real.

All three of them laughed, their bodies shook with it and they answered her thought.

Their answer was also a thought, one that formed in her head with their answer. "Earth people—people of this earth. That's who we are. Of course this is real. Look before you and believe your senses; we're standing right here in front of you. How can you deny us? You don't remember now, but you are us, and we are you." The thought contained so much more; the moment was fuller than words can explain. Jo accepted it instantly and knew it was true. She remembered something important. She remembered that she was on earth right now, but she wasn't staying here forever, just for this moment. She also knew that moment was a whole lifetime for her. Hours passed, in her memory—hours of bliss—where she visited her family, family that suddenly had vast new boundaries and definitions. Afterwards, she couldn't say how long they'd stayed or what specifically they'd talked about or done, but she knew some things that she didn't know before. She knew she could have gone with them and disappeared without a trace into the earth, could have stepped with them right out of this world. She knew there were still things she wanted to do and they'd agreed; she knew they were always here with her anyway, and she could lean on them whenever she wanted. It was an experience that uplifted her beyond where she'd ever been before, and when Newt drove in the next day she was as serene as could be.

The pipeline

Northern BC is being threatened with pipelines. There are so many pipelines being planned, the drawings look like sewer drawings.

One fellow gets our phone number and we agree to meet him and talk. He is an older man, very pleasant and well spoken, who has worked most his life for the petroleum industries. We sit outside at the picnic table for his visit. The wind is picking up and whistling in our ears, and he has to hang on to his papers to keep them from being blown away.

He explains that the pipelines will be closer than a mile to Fraser Lake and bordering our property. The pipeline he represents is interested in building the line to transport natural gas to a terminal at Kitimat where huge refrigeration units would cool the gas to a liquid form, reducing the volume and packaging it into a container similar to a propane bottle. The gas is for export.

He pulls out a map and holds it down on the table while he points out the proposed route. It intersects with an existing line that belongs to Pacific Northern Gas, but the right-of-way diverges at several points. There is an access route marked right across our property, and we point out that there is no right-of-way where his map says there is.

That doesn't bother him at all. He wants to get our permission for anyone associated with his company to use our property for exploration. He has a paper with him that he wants signed saying so.

There's a liability waiver, which he says protects us if they get hurt on our property.

He has answers to all our questions, except some of the important ones. The refrigeration units are power hogs, and he thinks there will be a new power line built from Prince George. That's odd: last time we checked Prince George wasn't a power-producing city. He doesn't mention Kemano Generating Station or the fact that Rio Tinto Alcan is in the process of finishing the second tunnel through Mount DuBose to divert more of our river towards the power plant, or that they're thinking of drilling a third.

He doesn't know how the gas is getting out of the ground, and the words "hydraulic fracturing"—or the short version, "fracking"—don't pass his lips. I mention my young friend who lives near Fort St. John who says they are having earthquakes and everyone thinks it's because of the fracking. The pipeline man is a better talker than a listener.

He explains how benign the project is, how it's a made-in-BC industry, and that we don't need federal approval, all we need to do is have a provincial review, and it is his forgone conclusion that the province will be a better place because of his company's investment. He says it's not like oil, which wrecks things if the pipeline has a breach; the gas will evaporate. He doesn't mention it may be a tad explosive.

We say, "Thanks for coming. You can leave the papers with us," and he tries a few more times to get us to sign on the spot. He infers that they may want to buy a chunk of our land and that we may be glad we co-operated. Finally, he goes. I file the papers.

Later on, a friend says that the pipeline people are like flies coming to rotten meat: they all want a feast on right-of-way, and then they'll smell nice enough that bigger companies will want to eat them in turn. They're one of the signs of something rotten.

... *Living in Endako*

When Newt had left Jo alone in the woods for three weeks, he'd gone to Vancouver and talked to his mother. He was the proverbial "apple of her eye," and it seemed she was willing to bankroll him endlessly. He'd confessed his disappointment in the mine, but she'd expected it and wasn't near as surprised as her son was. She gave him enough money to fix the Cat and he took it and went home to Endako to do the repairs before he returned to the mine.

When he got back to the Kootenays, it was only to pick up Jo and move back home to Endako. He had a small job land-clearing that he needed to start right away. He never did get back to serious mining; they came down in the summers, but it was more like a vacation. Some years they put a few yards of muck through the works, and some years they simply puttered about, getting things ready for the next time. Newt did small jobs with the Cat at home in Endako, small jobs that paid well, and Jo got a job working in the bush. Her job was bucking; running a chainsaw on the landing where sawlogs were skidded with their limbs still attached. The skidder was a big, rubber-tired machine, all four tires chained up with a giant set of formed steel chains. When the skidder dropped the trees, he'd turn around and run over them lengthwise with the blade skimming the bark, breaking off all the branches that stuck up. The ones on the bottom had mostly broken off while being skidded in, but the ones on the sides needed to be trimmed and so did the tops and butts. She'd fire up the chainsaw, knock off the remaining limbs, top the tree where she thought it measured five inches, and make a smooth cut at the butt, taking off any flare or splits while doing so. If it was a long skid then there was plenty of time, but if the trees were close to the landing, sometimes the skidder would have to wait till she was finished bucking the last drag before dropping the new one. She didn't like to keep him waiting at all, and she didn't like her quality report to have any errors, so the job was a tough one, with lots of plain hard work. Sometimes her arms ached at night so much she couldn't lie on them, and the trigger finger for the saw kept locking painfully into position, waking her up at night with the cramping.

"It's like getting a charley horse in your palm," she told Newt. He brought her home a book about natural remedies, and she started taking shark cartilage to try to combat the symptoms. She went to visit her Gramma GreyGrouse who gave her willow bark to brew before bed and told her to quit running a saw. She was too little for that kind of work, and it was telling her so.

Jo started doing beadwork, but not only the traditional kind where you bead patterns on leather or looms—her beadwork also went out in new directions. She started with a beaded curtain for her bedroom. Sometimes she still slept with Newt, but she had her own room where she kept all her supplies for crafts. Some were packed in a trunk that she'd fallen in love with and hauled around ever since: a big wooden sailor's trunk, wrapped with rusted metal strapping that was cut into swirling patterns of waves. It had a big, hinged clasp to close it and a metal ring that could be locked if one were inclined to lock things. Her bed was tall, with such long legs that she kept a little stepstool beside it. The space underneath was big, and the trunk fit nicely. She laid a long towel underneath, and when she wanted something in the trunk she simply tugged on the towel edge and the whole thing slid out on the smooth linoleum so the lid could be opened and the beads accessed. When she was in Vancouver she'd frequented bead stores and was always on the lookout for old necklaces whose beads she could recycle. She had a respectable bead stash in that trunk.

Jo incorporated patterns into the curtain, starting with the outside rows and working towards the centre. She had lots of beads: beyond the seed beads and recycled necklaces, she could pull out shells, wooden and bone beads, prisms and glass icicles, acrylic angels, and grapes. The curtain turned into artwork, pulling visitors in to peer and comment. The curtain gave her ideas for other projects. The contemplation of beads, the way a reflected rainbow prism dancing across the wall lifted her spirit simply by seeing it, made her want to make a curtain full of light. Jo felt that beads had a noble purpose, reminding us of beauty. It made her think of the earth people, and often while doing beadwork she'd smell that fresh earth smell and be reminded of the visit she'd had. She'd never told anyone about them; it still felt private. She loved that earthy first green grass smell that always made her think of them. Often she wondered if the visit had been real, always she chose to believe her senses and memory.

Jo never threw anything away that could be used, but she wasn't a hoarder. If she thought someone had a good use for something she had, she'd give it to them. If she went visiting, she'd always take some little gift. If someone came to see her, they would leave with a little gift. It was something she learned as a child: her dad would never go anywhere to visit without bringing a bottle. She absolutely knew that what went around came back around, and there was satisfaction in knowing it. That knowledge had been reinforced by her visit with the little people. She knew not to say bad things about people, knew the power of her word. Sometimes when a talkative visitor would be saying mean things about some other person, Jo felt the blackness behind their words, and she wanted to tell them to only say nice things. She learned to keep quiet. Newt had jumped on her after a visit with his friends when she'd countered every bad thing they'd said with a good thing. He'd told her she didn't have to be Pollyanna, that people could say whatever they wanted, and that she wasn't going to change opinions of people with closed minds and she should quit trying. After that, she'd listen and look at the corners, almost expecting the hand of fate to be visible. She grew intolerant of gossip; she simply didn't want to hear that shit anymore, and found it easier to walk off into the woods and let Newt deal with those kinds of people.

After ten years of living with Newt, she had a much clearer idea of who he was. What came clear to her was that Newt loved women, and pretty women the best. She knew he was divorced, but she didn't even know the name of his ex-wife, and he didn't talk about her or his marriage.

Newt began to have a hard time turning off the TV. He started living his life during commercial breaks. He lost interest in doing things, but was always full of praise for what Jo did. Jo knew he loved her, he'd told her so, but it was damned hard to feel appreciated when he would fasten all his charm on some other woman. He thought it was okay to flirt with everyone. He'd say, "For Christ's sake, Jo, I'm having a harmless conversation, getting to know another person." Jo remembered how jealousy felt from the other side, and she was determined not to pay attention to her own jealous thoughts. They felt darned uncomfortable from the inside, too.

Jo gave vent to her creative impulses, beading and quilting during the winters. Newt encouraged her: he slept under a quilt that she'd made on the top of a wool blanket, his old shirts living again as the pattern on the quilt.

... Seeing Jon

Newt worked with the Cat whenever he could. It wasn't too often, but it didn't matter so much because he always had money coming in from his mom. She sent regular cheques and sometimes bonus ones. Newt was generous with his mother's money; he bought people drinks in the bar and still drank Grand Marnier himself. He loved old luxury cars, and the one thing he still did was keep his Cadillac shiny and running well. Jo had to beg to get the garden disked every year, and though she wished he'd do it with a machine that compacted the soil a little less than the huge D8 he rattled over it, she didn't say. He didn't like being told how to do things, took it as criticism, and one year, in a fit of pique, he didn't till it at all. That year she turned the whole garden over by hand, and even though she was a little late planting, the garden thrived. Jo decided it didn't like being trampled with the Cat, so she mulched heavy in the fall and the next year it dug a little easier. She decided to never let him till it with the Cat again, and every time she found a worm she carried it over to the garden and told it, "Here's your new home." Every year the garden improved. She didn't need to buy potatoes anymore, and she had canning done for the winter.

Jo wasn't prepared to see Jon the day he stopped by. She was at the bar, not working but having coffee and chatting with the girl on duty, when he walked in. She recognized him immediately and froze to her stool. She hadn't seen him since the long-ago night of the fight. He knew her right away, walked directly over, smiled, held out his hand for a second, then thought better of it. "Oh, hell," he said and hugged her. She found herself hugging him back, tears welling to the surface. So many years, trickled away between them, so many memories struggling to surface, so much denied feeling pounding at her.

Her voice squeaked and sounded ridiculous to her own ears. "Jon." He backed off, kept in contact, his hand warm and reassuring on her arm. "I heard you lived here, Jo." She was caught by his eyes; they said so much more than his words. Jo stared at him and barely heard him say, "How are you doing, anyway?"

When the words finally penetrated, Jo shook her head, smiled a weak smile, glanced up again, then away. Her feelings were rolling around like a kaleidoscope, all bright and jumpy and falling against each other—smiling faces, heart connections, folding in on themselves and other images rolling up the sides. They'd been friends for a long time before they were more than that, and the intervening time shrank away and Jo touched the feelings of yesterday; seeing him was like seeing part of home. The bright colours coalesced and she relaxed. They talked about other things, and when she asked, "How 'bout you Jon, are you married?" and he nodded, she was good with it till he added, "She's not like you."

"Oh, Jon," she said, fully conscious of her friend taking in every word of their conversation. "Maybe you wouldn't like me now." He smiled, shook his head.

"It's nice to have friends," she smiled a "please" to him and he nodded. She still knew him well enough to read him. Hours passed while they caught up; he knew lots of her friends and where they were and what they were doing now. When he said he had to go she was surprised at how disappointed she felt, but when he said he'd see her again, he made it sound like a promise. She didn't tell Newt she saw Jon.

Ta'Kaiya Blaney

On Facebook people are talking about Idle No More. Some people have sent links and told others how to join. Some pictures of protests are posted and many opinions. Some decidedly racist comments are posted, and it's easy to see why some Natives are getting angry. Many people seem to think that Natives are living a life of leisure on the backs of the working class: "Our tax dollars support them"; "they don't have to work"; "they are provided for"; "they should have to work like every other Canadian"; "they should end reserves"; "if you live off the tax dollar, you should have to disclose all financial transactions" are all comments I read.

In conversation, people advance the opinion that history should be disregarded; they say, "That has nothing to do with you or me, what people did long ago. I work for a living; why should someone else live off my back? Why do I have to support them simply because they were born with a brown skin?"

Telling them that it's because when we disregard history we cannot learn from it sounds like preaching. Telling them that when our ancestors stole the land from them they promised that society would ensure they were provided for in perpetuity—something that the earth had previously ensured—is pointless because they wouldn't hear.

Telling them that the resources that are making Canadians rich don't really belong to Canada would make them mad. Saying colonizers appropriated all the land and left no resources for the indigenous people and that the basis for the ownership of this country is unfortunately unstable might get you into a big argument.

There are some more positive comments posted as well and the overall mood seems to be good. The movement may only be a venting mechanism so people can feel like they did something. Sometimes government will listen to the words of the Natives or an environmental group, and then after the people have had their say, the government says, "Thank-you" and goes and does what it wants to anyway. If anyone questions the move they say everyone already had their say.

Their words are spoken; they are simply given no weight.

One of the Facebook links is to a young Native girl named Ta'Kaiya Blaney, hailing from the west coast of BC. She has a video that is being shared. She is a beautiful young girl, and at eleven years old she is already an excellent speaker. She talks about how things used to be and how they are now. When she was ten years old, she travelled to the UN to plead her case for environmental changes. She thinks her trip was lip service only, that the heads of the world governments are not prepared to make the necessary changes, and they simply want to appear to be doing something, so they talk.

She is carrying the Idle No More message. She talks about how her grandparents would watch the tide recede, and then announce that the table was set, how they could walk out into the tide flats and eat fresh from the ocean's abundance. She says now those same places are not safe, and eating raw food from that same place may make you sick or even kill you because of the poisons from the industrial age.

Ta'Kaiya talks about the pipelines and how they will not be allowed. *She will not allow it!* There is hope. She is so clean, so young, she has no blemishes in her purity. That child is a leader! How strange it is that children are leading us. When before in the course of events have the adults had to learn from the children? Ask any grandparent living in Canada and you will find that the children have taught them how to use electronic devices; often the grandchildren know more than their elders.

... Jo leaves Newt

Newt's idea of freedom was tied up with driving. He loved to get behind the wheel and cruise the highway. At home, he would get restless and find himself pacing around, turning the TV from channel to channel and not finding anything interesting, trying to read a book and not being able to focus on the words. He called it "getting antsy," and his solution was to drive. He'd go visiting for the afternoon or evening. Sometimes Jo would go, sometimes not. She had her criteria for people she visited: they had to be able to laugh and have fun, she didn't like visiting sour people.

If she wanted to go out west for fishing or berry picking she'd catch the bus or drive her old pickup. Sometimes she'd catch a ride with someone, and Newt would come pick her up later. Their relationship was going downhill; they were together more from habit than mutual admiration. Jo could see that Newt talked the talk; he was well read and intelligent, and listening to him you'd think he was running full tilt between heavy equipment operating and mining. Every time he told the stories some of the details changed, and over time Jo thought he'd forgotten what really happened. His part was embellished and hers diminished till it sounded like she'd been the bull-cook. Sometimes she'd look at him, and if he'd catch her eye she would see an odd look in it, a hunted look that made her wonder. It was hard to respect him.

Other times, he'd surprise her with insights that she'd not suspected he had, or with a humorous remark that she would remember and laugh about again. Newt still knew how to be charming, how to creep into her room and into her bed, but those were things he did less and less.

The important day, the day that changed the world again for Jo, started lining up days before when Jo had taken the bus up to visit her Gramma, who was getting very frail and elderly. She'd come home a day earlier than planned. Jo got off the bus at the highway and walked in the short drive to the house; she noticed Newt's car in the driveway and knew he was home. She was hoping he'd remembered to water the garden; it was lush and the weather was hot. The front door was locked, unusual in itself, but she thought nothing more of it because the patio door was always open. She put her bag down by the door and walked around the corner; the garden caught her eye. It looked good, Newt must have watered it. She wandered over, pulled a carrot and wiped it on her pants, bit off the root end, spit it out, then crunched down on its sweetness while she surveyed the rest. In the silence she heard an odd noise and stopped chewing.

She couldn't quite make out what it was. It almost sounded like the grunt of a mother bear, and Jo automatically stepped towards the safety of the house, ears and eyes on full alert. She stood outside the patio door, her hand on the handle ready to step inside and listened again, only this time it was obvious that the sound was coming from inside the house. Her gaze swung to the interior. She could see through the open door of her bedroom and the sight froze her. Afterward, she didn't know how long she stood there watching Newt. He was nude and doing a sex dance with someone, she couldn't see who—all she could see were the legs wrapped around Newt's waist, opening and closing, opening and closing. Suddenly she felt like a peeping Tom, so she withdrew, backing away slowly at first while she was near the door and then fleeing in a run to the spruce tree at the edge of the woods. She sank down under the tree and sat there for the longest time, her back pushed into the tree trunk like she might absorb its strength that way. She watched the door, wondering the whole time, "Who?" Torn between hurt, betrayal, and anger: "How could he do that in my bed?"; "How long has this been going on?"; "That son of a bitch! What's he catching to give me later, unsuspecting?"; "Asshole!"

Afternoon turned into dusk, and still Jo sat under the tree. She saw the lights go on, saw figures walking around inside picking clothes off the floor and putting them back on, saw them sit at the table and have a drink, saw them clink their glasses in the air. Jo sat suspended in a sea of indecision. She knew she was at a crossroads and she was sensing all the directions she might take. All of them took off from here; here was where she no longer belonged. Some part of her thought, "That's what you get when you trust a man—told you!" You get either a crazy, jealous idiot or a person who betrays trust in a totally different way. The past reached out and grabbed her; she felt so alone, so not a real part of anyone's life. Tears of self-pity rolled down her cheeks and she made no move to wipe them away. She smelled damp earth.

Eventually, they put on their coats, momentarily disappeared from view, and she heard the door open. Jo saw Newt freeze when he spotted her bag, saw him look around and not see her in the advancing evening darkness. They didn't speak as they got in the car, but Jo knew who it was anyway. She didn't need to hear her; she recognized the flat-footed walk of Sadie, her supposed friend who was the waitress at the diner. Well, Sadie could darn well have him; she was more than welcome to him, in fact she wished her well with him. Maybe it was the shot Jo needed to kick her loose from Newt. She was going away permanently; there was no doubt about that. She let herself in to the house and looked around. Everywhere she saw things that used to mean something to her, but now all she saw was stuff. She didn't want any of it. She wanted her trunks, she had two of them now, and she wanted her clothes.

Jo had the duffel bags out and was going through her dresser drawers when Newt got back. He came in and leaned against the wall. He didn't say anything for the longest time, just kept watching her sort clothing. She said nothing either. If he was waiting for her to accuse him, then he was going to wait a long time. No need to state the obvious. She tried to focus all her attention on the task at hand, internal dialogue limited to "winter clothes in the green duffel bag, oh yeah, don't forget your boots; that top, doesn't really fit anymore, into the trunk; love that one, take it now. White duffel. Beads and craft supplies, all in the old trunk. Sewing projects, new trunk so they get that nice cedar smell. Blankets? I'm going to need blankets. I'm not touching that one they made out on; I'm not sleeping under them again. Get the ones from the closet, those new ones. Get the pillow."

Newt finally broke the silence. "Is there anything I can say?"

"No."

"I have to say it anyway—she means nothing to me."

Jo looked at him, shook her head, and let out an exasperated breath. "You idiot, that's the worst thing you could say. I might understand if you said you fell in love with her and couldn't help yourself, but to do that with someone who means nothing to you, that's fucking revolting."

"It's just sex. That's all. It's you I love."

"You got a damn funny way of showing that, Newt. Now will you get out of the way, cuz I am packing. I won't be darkening your door again."

"Ah, come on, Jo," he pleaded. "I really do love you. That was sex, nothing important. I won't do it anymore if it bothers you that much."

Jo hesitated. He actually was crying, the first tears she'd ever seen him shed. She sighed, her feelings battling it out. After a small silence she looked at him, spoke in a tiny voice. "Okay, Newt. One year. I'm giving you notice. You've got one year to convince me that it's important that I be here."

He came towards her with the clear intention of hugging her but she backed up, held up her arm in a warding-off gesture. "Don't think about touching me; you're not clean enough to touch me right now, and it ain't the kind of dirt you're gonna be able to wash off in the shower!" Jo slammed the door, stripped the bed of its blankets and replaced them with the ones she'd pulled from the closet.

It didn't take a year for Jo to find out that she had no respect left for Newt: it was already over. Now that she knew to watch she realized that Sadie was only one in a string of women that Newt was having sex with. Married women, women she never imagined would be coming to her old man for that reason, were coming. It was like she didn't exist, and she felt so belittled by them, by Newt and by them. The slow pot boiled over again in early spring. He'd been out for hours and when he walked in the door she could smell the sex on him.

The words turned ugly quickly, but soon Jo grew silent, she had nothing more to say. She recommenced her packing that had been interrupted the year before; she wandered about the house picking up little pieces of her life and tucking them into the trunk—the little jars of herbs in the cupboard that Newt would never use, a couple pots that were hers when she moved in, some towels and washcloths, a few dishrags. It wasn't much, and when she was done she had a tidy pile in the middle of her room: two travelling trunks and three duffel bags. It wasn't much to show for fifteen years. There were no traces of her left in the house, no pictures on the walls, nothing that said "Jo's house," and she realized it had never been hers—she had never stamped it, and no part of her was staying. A plan was forming in her head, a yearning to be where no one knew her, a way to start fresh, to be where she was before goddamn Newt showed up in her life. Later she'd say it was the time when she learned that if you want to be happy you'd better not depend on any other thing on the face of the earth to make you that way, the only way you can be happy is to do just that. *Be happy*. She was starting to be happy right then.

Newt left in the middle of the packing, and wasn't home to help her load things up. She threw the light things in the cab. The trunks were big and awkward; she wasn't sure how she was going to get them in the box of the truck. It had started snowing hard. She wished Newt was there to help her, and then she knew she didn't wish that at all. He was history, and from now on she'd be doing all things herself. So she used the pry bar and lifted one end of the trunk, slipped a blanket under it, and then by pushing, she could manoeuvre it out the door, across the porch, and down the two planks that she used to bridge the gap between the porch and the back of the pickup. At the last minute she remembered to get her saw and hardhat with the flip-down face screen. She threw them in the back of the pickup with the trunks and turned east on the highway. The snow was coming down thick and there wasn't much traffic. Visibility shrunk as she drew closer to Prince George. She slowed to a crawl but kept driving, turned north at the city and kept driving north. She stopped in a pullout to sleep for a few hours, tackled the Pine Pass in the daylight, and ate when she got to Chetwynd. She followed the Alaska Highway, turning left at Fort St. John and heading to Fort Nelson. The paper she'd read the day before had said they were short of workers there. At the time it seemed like a sign, and that's where she was heading. When she got tired she slept again in the truck, pulled over beside the highway, duffle bag for a pillow and covered up with a handmade quilt.

She drove for hours with nothing but her thoughts for company. Sometimes tears ran a silent course down her cheeks, and sometimes she smiled with relief. She renewed her vow—no more trusting anyone. She hadn't met anyone yet whom she could trust. Thoughts of Sam, of Dan and Gramma GreyGrouse she firmly pushed away—of course she trusted them, it was relationships that couldn't be trusted, and she was not going to be involved in any of them. Nope, never again. Well, unless he was perfect—then, who knew? Then she laughed at herself for qualifying "never" with "unless." When she got near towns, she'd turn the radio dial till she found a station clear enough to make out the words through the static, and sang along with the songs. In between were long contemplative hours. The snow stopped coming down and the highway was boring; it was too early in spring for any greenery, and the occasional hitchhiker she picked up was never going far.

The paper had not lied; in Fort Nelson they were desperate for workers. She got a job in the restaurant where she went to eat breakfast. By supper, she was working part-time, evenings and Sundays, waitressing. The owner of the restaurant pointed her toward a place to stay, a tiny basement suite consisting of a room, a bathroom and a tiny kitchen, furnished and hardly big enough to fit Jo's meagre worldly possessions. She liked it, and it was all hers. The next day she found another part-time job from the postings at the Manpower office, cleaning at the school from three till six on weekdays. It fit well with the first job, and when she saw another ad for cleaning work in the hotel during the mornings, her days were filled, and so was her much diminished bank account.

She knew she wouldn't get anything from Newt in the way of support, but it wasn't a sore spot because she expected nothing. Over the winter, she'd lent him most of her savings to fix his machine. She knew he didn't have the cash to repay her yet, but she figured it was like money in the bank. She knew Newt enough to know that he'd repay her sometime. They'd never married, never discussed marriage, and now that she knew he'd been finding sex outside the relationship, a whole bunch of other things became clear: all the hours he spent away from the claim, disappearing for days and weeks at a time; his visits to Vancouver to see his family—how much was real and how much lies? He was always so cheap with the money. All the gold they'd ever got from the claim was always his; he never shared his or his mother's dough with Jo. The only money Jo ever called hers was the money she made herself. She'd seldom had lots of money, but she always had some. In Fort Nelson, wages were high; suddenly she had lots of money, and in the first three months she saved ten grand.

Fort Nelson was a man's town—the men outnumbered the women by a large ratio. Jo attracted lots of male attention, and it was like a balm to her heart. She flirted with them all and accepted none; she was done with that shit. "Pretty to look at, but not to touch," she joked to Dan on the phone. Things weren't going too well for Dan: he and his wife weren't getting along, and there were little kids, and he was drinking, and so was she. Separately. Lots of times Jo felt helpless after she talked to him on the phone. He knew he was fighting himself but he couldn't seem to quit. For the first time in her life she knew she was stronger than Dan, and she tried to help him out, but it was tough to find the right words.

Winter in Fort Nelson was the coldest Jo had ever been. It wasn't the temperature so much as the wind. The wind was pervasive, the cold air tossed up and armed by the wind with a savage bite that penetrated layers of clothing. She still went for walks, fast ones to her jobs and back, but saying she enjoyed it would have been stretching the truth. Summer came late but it was fabulous, with the skies sunny for twenty-hour days, and the nights never dark as the glow of the sun still shone from behind the night skyline. The wind in summer was a blessing, blowing away the clouds of bugs. Summer was fabulous and short. Soon enough, the winds turned cold again and Jo started thinking about another winter in Fort Nelson. Suddenly, Vancouver sounded better than it ever had in her life. In September, she had the old pickup tuned up and new tires put on, then she loaded her bags and headed south. She didn't stop till she got to the coast, and then she thumbed through her little book of friendly phone numbers, found one she wanted to visit, and excitedly announced that she was there. "Yes, today! I am sitting in my truck beside the turnoff that brings me to you."

From Vancouver, she went east to the Kootenays and was visiting in the home of a friend when something happened that surprised her to the core. A stranger pulled into her friend's driveway, came to the door, and asked to speak to Josephine, who, he added, might be a visitor. Jo stood up and said, "That's me. Jo." She went to the door.

"I'm Hal Hobbe," he said, holding out his hand. "Can we talk? Outside?"

He didn't look familiar but her friends were right there, so Jo stepped outside and closed the door. "Do I know you?"

"No," he paused for a moment and then he plunged right in. "I need to talk to you: it's about your son, the one you gave up for adoption. I'm his father. We got him when you gave him up. We raised him; he's a fine young man, and I can't tell you how proud I am of him. I'm trying to do right by him; I wanted to find you and ask you to be a part of his life."

Jo just stared. Time warped. This man knew her son, said he's his father. His first father never even saw him, and his next father hurt him. This man loved her son—her son. She burst into tears, tears for her son and herself bottled up inside came bubbling out her eyes. She was totally embarrassed to be crying in front of a stranger, yet desperately wanting to hear more. "Part of his life!" Could it be true? She smiled through her tears, sniffing and shaking her head. "Don't mind me, it's just—just …"she trailed off.

"It's okay. I know it's a shock. I tried to practise what I was going to say to you, but I didn't say any of the things I practised."

Jo tried to smile, managed a shaky one. "It's such a surprise; I gave up trying to find him a long time ago."

He put his arm over her shoulder and gave her a quick squeeze, reassuring, buddy-style. He seemed so nice, so compassionate, and Jo liked him right away. They sat down outside at the picnic table and he told her how their boy had wanted to know who his real mother was since he was young, and always they had resisted telling him, how his wife didn't want him to find Jo; she thought it might prove to be a disappointment for the boy. He went on to tell her that he and his wife were separated, and because he always felt bad about not helping his son understand and come to terms with his past and his origins, he was trying to fix it now.

Jo was angry and hurt by the assumption that getting to know her might be a disappointment. "And what do you think, am I a disappointing find?" she asked, looking at him directly.

He shook his head, smiled a sad smile. "Please, Jo, I want to fix things. I want our boy to meet you. I want him to know where he comes from. There's so much we don't know. I'd like to be friends with you. He's a good son, he is smart as anything, and he's kind and good. You'll be so proud of him. You must have been very, very young."

"Fifteen, and I was epileptic." Jo answered on autopilot, her mind flying in a dozen different directions, the impossibility of ever finding her son turning into a probability. Here was her door back into the life of her son, and she was seized with gratitude. The man who had raised her son loved him, and he was proud of him; he said he was a wonderful boy, a happy boy. Unanswered, bottled-up questions could be asked, answers given. Jo felt such a surge of emotion that her usual reservations towards strangers were swept aside and she knew she'd met a kindred spirit, united by their love of the same boy.

Over the following weeks she alternated between elation that she'd found him again—or rather they'd found her—and anxiety that maybe he would be disappointed. It turned out that Hal had already journeyed to Telkwa and found Sam, convinced him of the need to find Jo and had been directed to the Kootenays by Sam. It was only by chance that Hal had found Jo: he'd been quizzing the lady in the post office and she'd sent him out to where he'd intercepted Jo. Hal had spent considerable time and effort tracking her down. He gave her his number and his brother's number and visited a few times, she talking about her life, he doing the same, filling her in on parts of their son's life. It was at times uncomfortable and sometimes she felt she was confirming the disappointing part of the story. She held out for the day she could touch her son and let him know how much she loved him. She planned some things she would say, would try to explain. She cried sometimes and laughed sometimes, but felt excited looking forward to the day of reunion.

A handwritten letter came to her in Grand Forks before she left, sent to Josephine Caplin, General Delivery. It was written in a flowery hand and Jo wondered who on earth could be writing to her. The letter was one page long and dashed her spirits to the ground.

It started off by assuring her that her gift of a son to them was appreciated beyond anything she could imagine. It went on to say that the author of the letter, she herself, was her son's mother and he had been raised right, that he was a Christian and knew his responsibilities. It said Hal was a sick man, he had been diagnosed as a manic depressive and was estranged from the family, and he could not presume to speak for her son. It said she understood he was offering to let her son meet Jo, but that her son was not interested in meeting her at this time, and if he ever was he would let her know personally. The letter closed with a biblical quotation. The letter dashed Jo's spirits down and her body went along for the ride; she huddled on the ground sobbing. She hadn't realized quite how much she wanted and needed her son till the possibility of meeting him had been held in front of her then snatched away. "Not interested" and "he'd let her know"—those two phrases cut her to the quick and she cried like she had cried the day she gave him away.

A place to rest

From the Kootenays, Jo travelled west again to Vancouver. She found out how many interesting things you could do in Vancouver with a little money. She went to all the places she had wanted to go, Science World and Stanley Park; she took friends out for meals, and they rode the buses together or she paid for gas for her friends to drive. She parked the truck in a friend's yard and then moved around, stayed with friends a few days here and a few days there. Months passed and suddenly Jo was tired of it, tired of feeling like a visitor ant in a busy hill. Everyone scurrying about doing their own tasks. She yearned to pick berries in the bush with the silence of the forest around her instead of beside the highway with the sounds and smells of traffic whizzing by. The purity of those highway frontage blackberries was questionable, grown in the haze of traffic exhaust, but she picked them anyway, justifying her actions with the thought that they were still a lot better than what you might buy in a store. More than any other thing, the thought of the berries in the fall in Hazelton pulled her up the highway one day, a yo-yo that ran out of recoil in the home of an old friend of her father's named Couy.

He was moving to the coast where his daughter lived, leaving the next month. Jo asked what he was doing with the trailer and he said he guessed it was a gift for the pack rats. She laughed with him and then offered to buy it. She had a little money left, not much, but better than the nothing he was going to get and she offered it all to him as a down payment. Within the hour they were signing up informal papers. "A conditional sale," he joked. "On condition of you paying me the rest, you own it. There's no hurry, girl, you pay me when you can. I'll be happier knowing someone's here. I was going to leave it empty and you know what that's like."

Jo did know what that was like, the north country reclaims that which man abandons. The forest slowly eats the wooden buildings that people leave empty: first the rodents move in, and then slowly the structure decomposes, leaving behind a mossy outline, sometimes a tin chimney and some rusted nails are all that remains. In a way she was saving the place and she was pretty happy with the deal.

The old guy had been a junk collector, and Jo spent weeks cleaning up the things he'd saved. Some needed to be hauled away, piles of old tires and various car parts. Some she saved, taking the nails out of planks stacked haphazardly in the yard and storing them in a pile beside the trailer. She found hidden treasures in the yard, old clumps of rhubarb and currant bushes. The yard was big, and Jo pictured it as she'd like it, with tall border plants screening her from the neighbours and a garden in the back. Owning her own place gave her a feeling of security that she'd been missing. She hardly recognized the feeling.

She had to limit the amount of reclamation she could do each day as her wrists and hands were often on fire from the work. It seemed she couldn't do any work anymore without hurting. Running the saw was almost out of the question, and if she spent an hour sawing wood then she'd spend a week with her right hand cramping up painfully, hurting all the way up to her elbow. If she hammered for more than a few minutes it would jar her nerves up to her shoulder and make her arm spastic—it was so annoying. She took some camp jobs because they paid well and were fairly easy to do. There wasn't much employment in the Hazeltons, and she no longer wanted to drive. The thought of a seizure while driving was scaring her from doing it. She slowly grew reacquainted with old friends and acquaintances she hadn't thought of in years and she made new friends fast. She invited very few to visit, and she didn't let anyone get too close. She had her guard up against the world.

Jo's friend from Stellaquo, Pam, phoned and asked if she'd like to go to Crabfest in Kincolith. The new highway made it possible to drive right to town and Jo jumped at the chance. She'd been wanting to drive there ever since the road was finished. She was so excited: Kincolith was her town—well, sort of—she'd never lived there and had never even visited, but it was her mother's town of origin. She had relatives there; her grandmother was gone, but she had other relatives there. She thought it might be awkward, not knowing who her cousins were. Pam joked with her not to sleep with any strangers because they might be relatives. Jo had always thought she'd like to visit Kincolith; the name always made her think of her mother.

When they got to town, the festival was in full swing, with crowds of people in the street, dancing to music belting out from the packed stage built at the end of the street. Musicians took turns all evening and festival organizers hyped up the crowd in between sets. The streets were lined with vendors, small booths where local crafters hawked their wares. There were jewelry makers, carvers, potters, and the whole gamut of home business wares. Jo loved looking around, trying to pick out the locals. She looked for people who looked like her. To her delight they were everywhere—short, round-faced people with perfect teeth and happy countenances—bustling around. She smiled at strangers in perfect recognition, thinking they could very well be her cousins.

Pam convinced her to go to the band office while she was there and introduce herself. She thought it was likely a good thing to do; after all, it was the band who claimed her. The visit went well till Pam announced that Jo had moved to Hazeltons, and she wondered if the band might give Jo a helping hand with financial aid. She winked at Jo as she said it. The friendly face closed and the business face looked out. That face said, "We have a policy for these sorts of issues. We tend to our people's needs, first and foremost, the ones who live here in our village. If your friend wants to move here where we can assist her, we can look into it."

"You mean that you'll only help her if she moves here?" Pam persisted.

"I didn't say that. This topic is one that we need to take up at another time. Maybe you'll come to the office during office hours?"

"I'm going home before Monday, is there a number I can call?" Jo asked.

She wrote the number and name down on the Crabfest itinerary, and they talked about it on the way home. Pam said, "It's not right. You're a band member, and they should have some way to help off-reserve people as well as the ones who live on."

Jo gave it some thought. She'd become used to being a Native in white society. Her skin colour had made her the recipient of all the negative things that society could throw at her—the discrimination and the unfairness built into the system—but she'd never received any of the benefits. She'd thought about it before: what it would be like to live in a village where everyone was Native? She'd decided she liked it the way it was; she liked being independent. She knew reserve politics and wanted nothing to do with them, didn't like the way elections pitted family against family, and she didn't like the nepotism involved in spreading the wealth of the reserves. She wasn't desperate enough to move to Kincolith and hope for crumbs. She was still getting by, taking camp cleaning jobs now and then, and doing other odd jobs, cleaning and waitressing. She was making ends meet and still saving some to pay out Couy.

"I don't know. It'd be nice to get some help from them, but I won't hold my breath," Jo said. "I'll phone the office in the week—it wasn't fair to lay that on her on the weekend when they're trying to organize all that other stuff. They were pretty busy."

Jo dismissed the topic; she had other things on her mind. "Did you see the size of the garbage dump? I'm not so sure it's a good thing having the road. The old guy I was talking to said, 'Before the road came, there was hardly no dump, and now it's huge and we go there to see the bears.' That's not fair to the bears or the people. And he said that the reason we couldn't get a room is because of all the fishermen. They're here for the salmon in the river, and he said they are a solid line of people there on the shore. If one person catches a fish they have to all run with him and take up their lines. No one local can even fit there anymore. Might be good for tourism, but who does tourism help? Do you think the average Joe would rather have tourists or be able to fish their river?"

"Well, the Crabfest was sure fun. I danced till my feet hurt. Do your feet hurt, Jo?"

"Yes, that was sure fun. I wouldn't live there, though. It sure feels like it's way out there, at the edge of the world."

"Even to be able to eat crab every day?" Pam laughed.

"Even for that!" Jo sighed with pleasure at the memory: piles of crab, reduced to empty rubble with the nutcrackers they'd used to crack them open to devour the succulent, butter-dripped morsels. She still felt a bit oily: they'd eaten till they couldn't fit anymore in their stomachs.

Jo phoned the band office at random times throughout the weeks that followed. At first she talked to the same person she'd talked to on the weekend, and then she was passed to another person who never was available when Jo called and never returned any calls when she left a message. Reading between the lines, she finally acknowledged that her band was not going to help her at all. Another friend told her that she thought the band paid a person a lump sum on retirement, even if they had never lived on reserve, but Jo didn't know how to find out if it was true. She sure hoped it was. It had been a pretty good summer; she was saving a bit of money from all the jobs she did, painting at one house and housecleaning at others. Jo practised living cheaply but well. She was getting a good sum set aside to pay for the house; she didn't intend to have that payment hanging over her head for any longer than strictly necessary.

Jo and Maria

Jo says Maria finished the welding course, and she did well. She passed everything and has a ticket saying she is a beginner welder. Maria's excited about getting a welding job, but there aren't many in Terrace, or none who want to hire her, so she's taking a job as a waitress again. Jo thinks she's doing good. The kids are getting out of school at the end of June, and they are taking a road trip down south. Jo wonders if it's all right to tell them to stay the night at our house. I tell her it sure is, and why doesn't she come with them? She can catch the bus back home. She agrees and we hang up saying, "See you soon."

They drive in with a different car this time, and with the luggage for all of them it's full. Maria unpacks Jo's luggage and a couple bags for her and the kids. She brings her guitar into the house with them. I grin at her. She is just as full of life as I remember, and when she grins at me I sense only her cheerfulness. The demons that drive her to drinking are well hidden. This time I am prepared: the bottle of Carolans on the table has four ounces in it, enough to serve a flavoured coffee each, but the rest of it is out of sight.

Our granddaughters are visiting as well; they are roughly the same age as Maria's girls. They hit it off instantly and disappear downstairs with the easy acceptance of children. They are deep into discussions on DS, a handheld electronic game that entrances them. There are hundreds of games that are accessories, and some of them so simple that even grandmothers could probably do it. I have that on the authority of an eleven-year-old—simple enough for a grandparent!

Where did these brilliant young people come from, feeling so superior at eleven? Maybe they are smarter; time will tell. Sometimes when I look around, I think overall that we sure could be a lot smarter in a lot of different ways. We could do a lot better job governing ourselves, and an age of peace would solve most our problems. Maybe they'll be smart enough for peace.

Maria's gained a bit of weight, but she's still pretty. She doesn't dress to hide her body, she dresses to be comfortable. She keeps us laughing throughout the meal, telling stories about welding school. She took the course through a local employment insurance incentive offered to people collecting from the fund. They paid her tuition and a small wage while she took the course, but didn't have follow-up job postings to place anyone, so what she learned appears to be going to waste. I show her the sunflowers my friend makes out of thin steel and ready rod. They easily get seventy-five bucks each at the farmers' markets, and there are dozens of other things a welder could make for gardens out of scrap metal. In the house I show her a magazine article I saved about how to make a petunia tree for the yard. I saw one in Clearwater in the bowl, it was shaped like a Christmas tree and up the trunk were welded diminishing rows of plates, topped with a single one. Tubing for automatic watering ran up the trunk and out each row of "branches." I had stopped the car in Clearwater to have a better look at it, and I couldn't at first figure out what kind of tree it was and had to laugh when I realized it was petunias. Who ever heard of a petunia tree? When I saw the design in a magazine article, I saved it. They retail at $250. I give the article to Maria, and she thanks me and tucks it into her purse.

The girls sleep downstairs on foamies and the couches, so Jo and Maria can have the rooms. We leave the children to their own devices; they only come upstairs for food and drinks. When we go to bed I check on them, and they're all still awake; they'll sleep in tomorrow. I get up early. So does Jo and we go outside quietly with our coffee to sit on the swing. Our house is built on a rise, and the sun hits us full on as soon as it peeks over the horizon. It's warm already, outside at dawn.

"This is my favourite spot in the whole world, this swing. Listen," says Jo.

I listen. The birds are singing, and in the distance we can hear an occasional mechanical crash, likely from the sawmill, maybe rail cars coupling or steel dropping on steel. Other than that it's quiet, not even any tractor noises. It's too early for haying and too late for planting. I grin at her. "Nice, eh?"

"You don't know how good you got it. In town it's never quiet, there's always dogs barking and cars going by, it's never quiet like this."

I do know how good this quiet is. "Yes I do. I used to live right beside the highway."

"Oh yeah, I forgot. It seems to me like you've always been here. It's hard to imagine you in any other spot. So you know what I mean, how nice it is to be away from all the noise. That's the only thing I don't like, not having quiet."

"Having to live in the downtown rat race of South Hazelton?" I tease.

Jo laughs. "You know what I mean."

"Let's pick the strawberries. Yesterday I noticed a few of them are ripe, probably enough to go with pancakes," I say when the coffee is done and Jo nods. In the garden where we can't be overheard, Jo says, "You're wasting your breath trying to get Maria to make garden stuff."

I look at her, surprised. "She really looked at the stuff like she'll remember. She might do it."

"Nope, she won't. She's not like us—if we want to do something we just go do it. It's not like that for other people. For Maria to do that she'd have to buy a welder, and where would she get the money, and then where would she do it? She lives in an apartment in Terrace. I can't see the management letting her weld there; she isn't even supposed to have a pet."

That makes me laugh, the mental picture of Maria hunkered down in the apartment with a welding arc lighting up the room for the girls to do their homework by, sparks flying. I go along with it. "She'd have to put out a sign: Caution, shield your eyes."

"And she'd need a cutting torch, and a pile of old steel to recycle. Maybe they'd let her store it in the lobby or the stairwell," Jo suggests and soon we're giggling like two idiots over our make-believe world where Maria runs her welding shop from her apartment. Pretty soon we don't talk anymore, but every once in a while one giggles and it makes the other join in automatically. It's a good way to spend these early hours, giggling over nothing in the strawberry patch with the song of the morning birds in the air. I've planted a row of silver birch beside the strawberries and they have grown about four feet a year and are big enough to be annoying with the amount of shade they produce. In the north we need all the sunshine we can capture and the birch are not helping, though they are beautiful white trees already at four years old. The sapsuckers, male and female, are busy tapping the trees, about eye level. They make concentric rings of holes around the trunks of the tree, all about the same diameter. The tree bleeds out there and both the birds and the ants are happy about the tree wounds. Deeper in the woods, I've seen a nest of bees using the sapsucker holes as entryways to their home; the sapsuckers are a firm part of the cycle and I don't care that they are wounding the trees. Maybe they know the trees are in the wrong spot. The pair of birds are friendly. They land close by and play peek-a-boo around the tree trunks. Jo is thrilled; she starts making their own noises back at them and it seems like they are having a real conversation. The birds quit being shy and come right out towards her, jumping down the branch a few inches at a time. I stay really quiet and they come really close, and then flit off together and land further away, talking to each other steadily.

Jo laughs. "I wonder what I said? They're probably over there saying, 'The nerve of her! Did you hear what she said!'"

"That's pretty good bird talk. How'd you learn to do that?"

She laughs again. "Another holdover from my days alone in the bush. I always had a connection to birds. At home I feed them in the front yard. I stood a spool on its end—you know those big ones they wrap cable on? I make it a three-tier feeder, and it's a free-for-all. The birds chase each other off and there's a definite pecking order, even with the same kind of birds. I grow lots of sunflowers, last year over a hundred, and I put them face-up on the spool. I buy big bags of the store seeds. They eat an incredible amount."

"I hung a bird feeder on the deck one year, and then I moved it to the woodshed and then I didn't fill it," I say. "They made such a mess between flinging the seeds and pooping, I wondered why anyone would go to the bother. For me, it's okay if they stay living in the woods."

"I like to see them," Jo says. "I can watch them for hours. You can't put the feeder in your own space. You have to put it close enough to see but far enough that the mess doesn't bother you. I put mine where I want the sunflowers to grow the next year. In the spring, you roll the spool aside and compost around where the outside was because the seeds are planted there and it's already fertilized with bird doo-doo. Then you can plant squashes or pumpkins or something in the middle. Works good."

"Do you know what all their names are?"

"The birds? Most of them. And I recognize most of their calls. Hear that? That squawking call? That's the pileated woodpecker, you know, the big one? They like ants the best, but they come to the feeder sometimes just to look around like they're curious as to what the fuss is all about. Sometimes the birds have little turf wars. Mostly it's just dancing and posturing, they hardly ever fight. But one day I was watching a little flock of chickadees eating away at the feeder, and before I even saw the crow coming the birds flew away, all but one who was a little late on the takeoff. That crow caught that little bird in mid-air: one minute he was flying, the next he was gone."

"Gives a whole new meaning to bird feeder, eh?"

"Janet!" Jo doesn't like that. "There is a guy down the street who feeds the birds too, but he only likes the little birds. He has a BB gun and if the crows or the magpies come he shoots at them. He thinks the BBs just scare them, but I know they have thin skin and that the BBs stick in them." Tears come into her eyes. "It's not fair: lure them in with food, then shoot at them. I found a dead magpie when I was walking, I bet he wounded it and it died slow."

The memory is making her cry in earnest, but at the same time she is starting to laugh. "Honestly, that's what I'm like lately, laughing one minute, crying the next." She shakes her head, sniffs a bit more, then determinedly starts talking about happy things. I don't think too much of it, it's part of being fifty and menopausal and facing another change in life. No longer able to conceive, it's a thing that strikes us all differently, but a thing that all women face. It seems like the more a woman has identified with motherhood, the more her self-image is tied up in that role, the harder it is to let go of.

"Age brings wisdom," I say to her and she nods agreement. "If it doesn't you'll die stupid," she says and we both start giggling again.

The kids straggle upstairs when we yell "breakfast." One of my granddaughters doesn't like pancakes so we make eggs as well. They all eat well, and they want to go outside and ride the horse. We have one old saddle horse and one colt who likes to buck, so he's not fit to ride. The girls take turns on the old horse bareback, then they double. Even though he's thirty, he still knows when a green rider is on his back so I lead him around with the halter. The girls don't care, they are thrilled to pieces to be sitting on a horse. It's the first time Maria's kids have been on one. I let him trot a bit, and they lose balance and fall off. They're not hurt: dignity maybe, but they want back on. I let them lead each other when I get tired, and they spend a couple hours riding. Finally, I take pity on the old boy and call them in. They crowd around petting him, and when I take off the halter he tosses his head, pivots, and takes off at a run. After a couple strides he ducks his head, kicks up behind, and lets out a big fart while he does it. The girls go into hysterics, and he shakes his head like he just showed them something and trots off. We all go in, laughing.

Maria and the girls leave shortly after lunch. They only have to make it to Williams Lake by evening so they have plenty of time. Jo is going to stay the weekend, and then she's going housesitting by Endako.

She gets home a few weeks later and is settling down to some serious garden harvesting when we talk. Jo sounds despondent. Maria had been down to see her on the weekend with the girls. She kept drinking all weekend, and when Jo and the girls came back from a long walk, Maria wasn't there. It turned out she was visiting the people down the street. The girls spoke to her, asking her to please quit drinking, and she got mad at them. Jo's not too impressed. She's sure Maria's not telling her the truth about all the bruises, but she encouraged the girls to speak of home and neither one said their mom was getting beat up, so maybe she did get them some other way. She thinks Maria is not facing herself, that she's turning face every way but the one needed. Jo's worried about the girls.

"I know what it's like, watching someone drinking all the time. It's not good for a kid to see that, it takes away so much else. It's such a shame."

178 — *Not My Fate*

"How are they, anyway? The girls, I mean? Apart from all that."

"When you're that age, there is no apart. They've already been hurt a lot by their dad, and they need her to be strong. But they're basically good, happy girls. We played dress-up in the fancy clothes and made tea. If those were my girls I'd never drink. I'd take way better care of them."

"Did she get a welding job?"

"No, apparently there are lots of people with those tickets. They are the lowest of three levels of welders and all the jobs are for people with tickets at the next level up or something."

"I thought there were tons of jobs at Rupert. Is it too far to drive?" My lips are going without my brain in gear. Of course it would be a very bad idea to encourage Maria to drive! Even through suggestion.

"Yeah, over kind of a crappy road, and the mine jobs are all camp, and then what about the girls?"

"So what's she doing?"

"Waitressing."

"She's probably a good waitress, she's so happy and friendly."

Jo says, "I wish I could keep them girls. Just for a while, I'd sure try to treat them good."

"Kids are expensive. It costs a lot to keep them clothed and fed. Let alone all the stuff they want."

"Not them two, Janet. It doesn't take much to make them happy. They don't have the DS's and the phones like your grandkids do. They're happy with simpler things."

It makes me so sad to think of the girls wanting and I understand Jo's urge to look after them. Once, she told me that everyone has to look after someone else. It doesn't matter how low you were on the totem pole, it was every person's responsibility to look around at someone who was wanting and ask themselves if they could help. She says the best way to help yourself is to help someone else. So I know what she means, and I don't think it's a good idea, not for her. It makes me wonder. "Do you think they're not safe?"

"Maria took them away from their dad when he was hurting them, so I think they'd tell her now if anyone was. Although she didn't believe their older sister when she told! She'd have saved those two a world of grief if she believed it the first time she got told."

"Did he get charged?"

"They still have to go to court for it. It hasn't happened yet. I think there is a restraining order or something till then. It's just gross, you know. He can't get at them anymore but he can get at the rest of the world. One guy like that, he can bruise up a lot of lives before he's done." Her voice cracks and there she is, crying on the phone. Shit.

"You can't save the world, Jo."

"Oh, I know I can't, it's wishful thinking. It makes me so sad, I've had a couple good cries since they left. I can't deal with her anymore, she's too hard to have as a friend. I think next time she wants to come I can't be at home. Even if I am."

We get on to other subjects, seed catalogues and who has pony tail amaranths, and whether the giant hogweed is the same thing we call cow parsnip and eat the young stems of in the spring. She says it's not the same, and I say it is. She says this new kind has stinging stuff on the stem, and I say so does cow parsnip, and she's sure she's right, and I'm sure I'm right. We both agree to find out more about it and compare notes again. I hang up the phone and hunt through all the plant ID books I have. Even here in the interior cow parsnip is every-where apparent. A drive down almost any back road in the fall will present you with the parsnip's showy leaves and umbrella clusters of white blossoms. At this stage if you try to harvest them you may get a serious skin reaction; they grow up to ten feet tall in moist conditions and are perennials, growing each year's enormous plant from the last year's root. I'm sure this plant is the same one identified on the news as "giant hogweed." There are two women in white suits who are making it their business to stamp out this plant in BC. It strikes my funny bone, this mental picture of the two in suits with machetes and paper masks and safety glasses. It's entirely up to my imagination to supply their looks, I only got this story second-hand from Jo, who saw it on the news. Anyway, good luck to them.

The next time I talk to her she's in a better frame of mind about Maria and the girls. The last visit she sent them home with a case of fish and some huckleberries. She did her best by them and now it's up to Maria. "Some friends, they use you up," Jo declares and renews her pledge to not be home again, not for a while at least. She talks tough but odds are Maria will be back in her life again pretty quick.

A couple months go by. We don't mention Maria, and then suddenly, "I knew it! He was knocking her around. This time there was no mistaking it, the girls even know. She phoned here but I wasn't going to be home, so she came down here to her mother's place instead and one of our other friends talked to her. She left him, and that's what counts."

Jo wonders out loud what it will be like for Maria to heal and quit drinking, and look back on motherhood. "She sure hasn't broken many cycles. Pretty well everything that happened to her, has happened to her kids. She's simply not a strong person, Oh, I know she comes across as being strong, but basically she's not." Jo is keeping her distance, only telephone visits, a quite conscious decision on her part.

A few weeks later Maria is back in the news. "She went back—he was sorry! Does this sound fucking familiar? Aren't they all sorry?" Jo is furious. "What the hell message is she giving to the kids with that? This takes the cake! This is about the stupidest thing she's ever done! She pisses me off so bad!"

I let her rant, giving an occasional *mm hm* of agreement. "If it's okay to forgive that once, then it's okay to forgive it a dozen times. Or a hundred. She thinks there's no lasting damage, she's sadly mistaken!" Jo's so angry with Maria that she says she's never even going to talk to her on the phone again. She's going to cut her out of her life. When she thinks of the girls she cries. "They'll know me when they're adults, they'll know how special I think they are," she sobs. I know she's too kind-hearted to be mad at Maria forever, so I'm not surprised when later on in the spring she says she's had a visit from Maria, who is way better, left that mean guy behind and is thinking of moving back, and Jo has gotten over being mad at her. Being mad at her doesn't do anyone any good. She's going to "reserve judgement" she says with a laugh.

Reserving judgement

Jo is in a blue mood. Being me, I try to make her laugh about something, anything. She is half-hearted about being happy, so I dig around and try to reason away her reasons for being in a sad mood. Turns out there's a lot of things combining to make her unhappy— the primary one she doesn't explain, but she holds the phone by the bucket that's going *plink, plink, plink* and I know right away it's not a leaky sink. I've got nothing to say to cheer her up on that issue. "Hurry up summer," I urge. Her brother Sam is another serious worry for her. I've never met her brother, and have this idea in my head of a male Jo, but sometimes when I'm talking to her I think my picture is totally wrong. He sounds like a hurting unit, sometimes walking around with so much suppressed anger that he shakes. She says people looking at him sometimes think he's not all there, and he gets bullied, at work and in town. The cops at the station, they know he doesn't drink and when sometimes he gets picked up by new guys they never book him, just let him go with apologies and warnings to go home. He isn't working right now because he got hurt at work and is on short-term disability and he doesn't know what to do with himself. The cops have made it plain that he's not supposed to hang out downtown. Jo is trying to get him interested in making things. That's how she gets through the winters, getting lost in the creative mood. It doesn't matter if it's quilting or beadwork, making stuff fills up the empty hours. He makes cedar planter boxes. He made some for himself last year, and Jo says she'll buy him the wood if she needs to so he can make them commercially. She thinks they'll sell at the farmers' market or in a garden centre.

Even mentioning Oprah doesn't do it. One of Oprah's schools is being mismanaged and even Oprah's in a bad mood.

I can't think of how to talk her out of that worry. "You can't save the whole world," I say.

"You can sure try to save your little corner of it," she tells me and laughs, a genuine laugh, and suddenly she is in a good mood. She thanks me and I feel like a human placebo.

Edmonton

Jo got a surprising call from her brother Dan. He was in jail. He'd been in for a while: his drinking and carousing finally came to a head and landed him there. It was time for parole and he needed to have a responsible family member stay with him for a minimum of three months as a condition of his release. He was going to walk the healing path sober, and he phoned Jo to see if she would be his support person.

"I don't know, Dan, come live in a city? I don't really do cities."

"There's isn't anyone else I can ask. Can you think about it for a while?" In her head Jo ran the list of family members, responsible ones who could drop everything and leave, and saw what he meant. "For you, I will do it. When?"

"If I can say you'll be the one and they approve, it'll only be a couple weeks. I'll keep in touch."

Jo was approved, and she went to Edmonton in midwinter. Her brother was released and he immediately went back to his old job as an auto mechanic. What was new was that Dan was sober every day, and in order to stay that way he decided on a regimen of support group meetings. Jo accompanied him to ninety meetings in ninety days, a real eye opener for her. She realized that no matter how bad you think you've had it, there is always someone who's had worse. The stories she heard went straight to her heart, and by the time she was halfway through her stay in the city she was greeting people on the street by their first names.

They moved into an apartment on the third floor of an apartment tower, and Dan relearned how to live soberly. Dan is light-skinned, medium height, with long dark hair usually confined in a braid. He's good looking and charismatic and he and Jo enjoyed the time renewing their bonds. While he was away at work Jo took the opportunity to cruise the city within walking distance. The apartment was fairly central in the city, and Jo found a health food store she really liked and, on the same street, a combined second-hand book and clothing store. There was one store that sold only beads and jewelry supplies, expensive but oh, so gorgeous.

Laughing about herself in the bead store, she told Dan that evening, "No wonder it was so easy to trade our valuables for trinkets and beads. I still want at least one of every kind of bead in that store. I'm like a pack rat: the bling catches my eye."

One of the places Jo liked to walk was down a main street, four blocks north of the apartment. When she walked down that street, people turned and looked; they smiled and waved; they were so friendly. Once, she walked out to the meridian to cross and two cars stopped to see if she needed a lift. Always people waved, and always she caught the eyes of strangers who smiled. It was puzzling but very nice. She made herself a route, past the stores she liked and through the street she liked, making a circle and arriving back at the apartment. She'd done it for several weeks before she spoke to Dan about it. She said how nice the people were on that street, as opposed to the averted eyes and hurrying people on other streets. Dan's eyes narrowed. "Say that again—where were you walking?"

Jo explained. She'd read all the street signs and she knew exactly where she'd walked. Dan started whooping with laughter, holding his stomach and collapsing on the couch. "Oh, Jo, they think you're working the streets. When they stopped they wanted to pick you up, like—you know!"

"No way!"

"Yes, Jo, you could have been making lots of money," he teased.

"Why didn't you tell me?"

"I never thought about it. Didn't you notice?"

Jo reflected. "I noticed people dressed up, but so am I! It doesn't mean you are a street-worker just because you have a dress on."

"Believe me, if you want to get a hook-up; that is the place you'd drive by," Dan assured her. Jo never took that route again; she made a different circle.

By the time the three months had passed, along with the meaner part of the winter, Jo was glad to be leaving the city. The meetings had taught her some things too. She could see that people created their own dramas, and she was determined to try to be the best person she could possibly be.

"I love you, brother. You are a good man and I know things are going to go better for you from now on," she told Dan when she left. "Phone me every day. I'll be at Janet's, and then at Rene's. I'll be there for six weeks, then home."

The people in your life

Jo comes to visit, and we talk her into coming to the bar with us. That's a major deal in itself. As she gets older, she gets more protective of her personal space. She keeps the gate closed in her yard at home, and it sends a message to passersby that is the opposite of welcoming. If she sees someone looking in she'll wave, but often as not then she'll move to where they can't see her, though she can often still see them. She's kind of like a deer that way, melding into the garden like a deer in the bush, then peeking through the foliage. Her yard is a sight to see, and no one can blame passersby for stopping and looking. All those bales of hay have composted. Jo threw soil on them and the earthworms did the rest. There isn't even any straw when she digs her shovel in. The decomposed bales are now hillocks of soil all over the yard, deep rich compost on top of sandy loam. In these mounds are planted perennials—show-stopper poppies, and peonies, Bridal Veil spirea, flowering trees, creeping vines and raspberries ten feet tall, strawberries and rhubarb, huge Jerusalem artichokes, delphiniums, horseradish, and celeriac—all decorating the front yard. There is no longer any lawn. Some grasses are growing in clumps four feet tall and some are trimmed into paths. Around the bases of the perennials are lettuce and radish, spinach and brassicas, all mixed together with wild abandon. The grass along the wire fence is six feet high, interspersed with trees and shrubs that block the view of the neighbours, except for one open space on each side where you can see glimpses of other yards, and one in the front, where the people stop and stare in. At first Jo didn't like people stopping and staring but she has become accustomed to it as she knows she'd stop and look if she saw another yard like hers, and furthermore she'd likely knock at the gate and ask to look closer.

It's fun dressing up to go out with Jo. She will wear her straw hat to the pub. After all, it's got black lace all around the brim, top and bottom, and is an all-occasion hat. And the hair must be braided just so. She doesn't want to look like Heidi. Her hair is getting long, to the small of her back; in the last few years it has turned white, but the kind of white that almost glows in the dark, sort of like negative hair. I like braiding it, turning the braid up in a tidy row down her head and out into the wispy ends. Today I notice that there is a big area on the back of her head that has turned black again. I exclaim with surprise and she grins at me like she has pulled a fast one. "I know!"

"How? I'm simply not going to believe you've found the fountain of youth and drank from it."

"No—it's something much simpler. Krill oil."

"What are krill?"

"I think they're sort of like shrimp. You should look them up."

"Later. Remind me."

I tie the end of her braids with a teeny elastic, and she pulls each braid forward and makes a long wrap around it with a thin leather lace, then ties it so it stays flat. She wants us to wear dresses but I refuse: the closest I'll go is leggings and a long shirt, vest overtop. I point out that it's almost like a dress and she nods and comes out in a long skirt, a short top that barely reaches her waist and a vest topping it off. We smile at each other and tell Rick he is one lucky man, getting to take us both out.

At the bar, Rick goes off with the musicians: they're all meeting here to jam and happy to see each other. As soon as we get there, they forget we exist unless they need us to harmonize, and then they might remember. Sometimes they are annoyed if we get too loud, and sometimes we get pretty loud trying to visit overtop the music. We're there at cross purposes. You never know who you're going to see at the bar and this night is no exception. Whenever the door opens everyone's eyes swivel around to it. There isn't much traffic, mostly off-sales, people dropping in to buy a box of beer. The music attracts a few who stay to listen and some stay all night.

Jo and I each have had one drink and about five coffees. Both of us are buzzed, and we tell all the musicians how wonderful they sounded and help pack up. They are all amplified, all packing their own systems that they patch together. Rick has a big old-fashioned board and amps, but it's a big hassle to take it apart and set up, and he only uses it if it's some big occasion. The other stuff is bulky

186 — Not My Fate

enough, and by the time we get the amp and its stand, the mic stand, the guitar and the accordion, the bag with all the accessories and the three of us in the pickup cab, it's entirely full. Rick sits in the middle on the way home and we tease him about being the thorn between the roses.

In the morning we look up krill oil. Like so many things now, we find there are good things and bad about krill. They do indeed look like shrimp, and some scientists believe that they comprise the largest biomass in the world. They are one step up the food chain from plankton and are found primarily in the Antarctic and off the Pacific coastline of Canada and Japan; they are harvested commercially to make the krill oil as well as for aquaculture; and they are harvested to feed to farmed fish. The oil is important for humans because it has the ability to reduce bad cholesterol at the same time that it builds good and also because it contains an antioxidant called astaxanthin which does something in the brain that other oils don't.

Krill is the main source of food for penguins, seals, and whales, and a whole lot of other creatures swimming through the ocean. There is some question about sustainable harvest; some people are concerned that humans are harvesting so much krill that the other creatures will go hungry.

"There are simply too many people," I say.

"Not so!" Jo says. "Everyone could have a good life if the world stopped fighting. It's mostly the governments fighting, not the people."

"And people are just people everywhere; they have the same wants, the same basic needs as everyone else. Give a person love, food, and shelter, and what more can they want?"

Jo grins. "Electricity, flat-screen TV's, hot running water, big cars and gas, holidays in foreign countries, dump truck loads of compost—to name a few!"

I'm feeling guilty about her list: except for the flat-screen TV, it's me. I say this and she laughs some more. "It's me, too," she declares, but there are a few things on the list that don't apply to her. She lives a tiny footprint, and doesn't even have a car. Although she still depends on vehicles to get her about, they're not her own. "But what's the alternative? Going back to the horse and buggy days? Could we?"

"I don't think we can go backwards and we sure can't go on the way we're going."

"Well I know one thing we can do. What everybody can do— they can learn how to grow enough food, so if the trucks and the trains stopped coming, at least we wouldn't starve."

"That's for sure," I agree wholeheartedly. We're not food self-sufficient, and if the supply chain broke lots of people would go hungry. There aren't too many people left from the hunter/gatherer era that even have the skills to hunt their food. Everything for life is right here, in the woods, but who can recognize it? Who knows what's safe to eat? Sometimes it's the difference between life and death, and eating the wrong things can kill you.

Jo says, "In older times people here didn't grow things, they gathered. Team that up with growing food and there would be enough. Food wouldn't need to be the deciding factor—you and I both know we can grow enough food to last the winter, probably enough for a few families."

I try to picture a future without the supply run up the highway, getting fruit and vegetables from China and South America and New Zealand, without homo milk delivered sterilized. This area is rich in cows and hay farms. I say, "We could get meat from the farmers. There are more cows than wild things."

"How many cows would there be if there weren't machines to make the hay?

"Yes, that's true," I concede. "The cows can't eat trees and shrubs like moose can." Too bad we don't farm moose or deer; they can at least live through the winter here, unlike cows. The first winter they'd all die. Moose can do something else cows can't do. They can jump so high it would take about a ten-foot fence to contain them; however, they can get just as tame as a cow. Friends of ours in Alberta took us out to the foothills to visit their old folks who had a tame moose; they got it when it was a baby, orphaned with a broken leg. They took it home, splinted the leg, and raised it like a pet. The moose was so tame it came inside the cabin. They could tie it up and pack things on it.

We grin at each other, both pleased to be solving the food crisis.

Jo says, "It's all so stupid, what's happening now—all the money governments spend on fighting. If they just took that money and all those fighting people and said, 'how about now you learn to grow things and feed other people instead of killing them', then the world would sure be a better place."

Newt's final chapter

In small communities almost everyone gossips. Some do it good-naturedly, some spitefully, but there isn't too much that doesn't get chewed over by the public maw. News of Newt gets handed around: he's been spotted in the old folks' home at Christmastime, but there isn't any room there; he's in a visitor's bed. He's there on what's called a "respite," to give the primary caretaker a break, often a much needed one. Sadie took him back home when she needed to, but then a few months later he's back in. There still is no room for him. It's kind of sad to say, but to get in the home you have to wait till someone dies.

He's demented now, quite out of his mind. At the door of the old folks' home he sits and tells visitors if they wait, he'll give them a ride because he's waiting for them to bring the car around. I guess he's been patiently waiting for the car-hop to bring his car around for days; time must have a different feeling for him now. Sometimes he gives up on the car coming, but it makes him angry, he's much grumpier without his rational mind, maybe in some way he knows he's been caged. Sadie has her hands full trying to look after him; she'll sure have to hide the keys, and no wonder she needs a break now and then. He needs full-time care.

Jo says she doesn't feel sorry for him. "Where he is, that's where he put himself. Look at him, never had do anything but look good and be needy. He got everything given to him, and he squandered it all. He could have been happy, could have stayed in his own mind. That's a choice—I think he made a deliberate choice to withdraw from everything. Remember when he kept saying he couldn't remember anything when he was remembering everything? He was hypnotizing himself to forget, and sure enough it didn't take long. He put himself where he is. I've been in their house, and I know how they treated each other. It wasn't nice—they weren't kind to each other. But you know what? They deserve each other. They both made choices that got them right where they are today." She changes the subject.

"Do you know that Native people are the fastest-growing segment of the Canadian population? Why do you think that is?"

I don't have an answer for that one for a couple days, and then it comes to me. Maybe it's in answer to majority rule—in a few short generations the numbers will be high enough to rule. I advance this opinion to Jo and she laughs and laughs.

Maria has moved back to Hazelton and she visits Jo often. We wonder if Maria will ever change, because she seems to keep treading the same wheel, tromping the same circles round and round. I ask Jo if she thinks Maria will ever walk the healing path, or if she'll be content to go on like she is till she's old, then dead.

"I'll be mighty surprised and very happy if she ever changes. She's kind of like Newt in that respect; she keeps treating herself to things that she knows are self-destructive. I don't know if she is strong enough to change." Her face turns serious. "You know, it's part of the cycle of life, this facing your demons and deciding who you are with them staring back at you. Even the Christians know that; they say the sins of the fathers are visited on the children."

I know this is true, the way childhood experiences affect adult behaviour. Something that happens to a child will direct the actions of that adult decades later. The Toltecs call it "living in the dream"; they say that every person has the capability of transcending the child within. When that child is hurting the adult, that's a sign to wake up and be alert. Everybody grows, everybody learns—the thing that sets exceptional people apart is that they change the parts that they don't like. Childhood sets the scene for those demons the adult has to confront and some end up with ugly.

The people who learn from the past, who have taken a clear look backwards and learned from what may be called the "mistakes," they are the exceptional people.

The country that looks at history and decides to learn from what may be called the "mistakes," that's the exceptional country.

Time goes on and things change, sometimes for the better, and some lessons stick. Jo's brother Dan has learned to stay clean and help others; Sam's wife also decided to walk the sober path. Governments and churches can reflect and apologize, although the true value of those apologies has yet to be seen.

I look at Jo and think of the demons that plagued her, and I see no trace of them. She has laugh lines around her eyes, and in my mind her face smiles. There are still things she has to resolve, and she has the daily struggle with life that most of us do, but she does it with a good nature. She's broken the chains of the past and strengthened the future with her choices. She's a survivor.

I'm thinking all these noble thoughts—she's thinking of more mundane matters. "Hey, what do you think about this idea? What if I get an old piece of carpet and lay it on the trailer roof, so it insulates it a bit more. Do you think the condensation will stop?"

"You go girl!" I tell her and we both laugh.

PHOTO BY WALLACE STUDIOS, VANDERHOOF BC

JANET ROMAIN is Métis-Canadian. She was born in Vancouver, but has lived most of her life in northern BC. She worked in a variety of jobs from short-order cook to lumber grader, but eventually bought land out in the country. She has three grown children and currently lives with her husband near Fort Fraser. She is surrounded by gardens and wildlife, just a stone's throw from where she grew up. *Not My Fate: The Story of a Nisga'a Survivor* is her second book with Caitlin Press.